MANAGEMENT OF CHILDREN AND ADOLESCENTS WITH ATTENTION DEFICIT–HYPERACTIVITY DISORDER

THIRD EDITION

RONALD J. FRIEDMAN

GUY T. DOYAL

pro·ed

8700 Shoal Creek Boulevard
Austin, Texas 78757

About the Authors

Dr. Ronald J. Friedman and Dr. Guy T. Doyal are child psychologists. In addition to their extensive clinical experience, they have both been university professors involved in the training of psychologists and physicians. Dr. Friedman is available to present seminars and workshops for professionals and parents. See the last page of this book for details. Dr. Doyal is professor and former head of the Department of Educational Psychology at Wayne State University in Detroit.

Cover design by Mark A. Doyal

Library of Congress Cataloging-in-Publication Data

Friedman, Ronald J.
    Management of children and adolescents with attention deficit
    -hyperactivity disorder / Ronald J. Friedman & Guy T. Doyal. — 3rd
    ed.
        p.   cm.
    Rev. ed. of: Attention deficit disorder and hyperactivity. 2nd ed.
    c1987.
    Includes bibliographical references and index.
    ISBN 0-89079-532-0
    1. Attention-deficit hyperactivity disorder.   I. Doyal, Guy T.
II. Friedman, Ronald J.   Attention deficit disorder and
hyperactivity.   III. Title.
    [DNLM: 1. Attention Deficit Disorder with Hyperactivity—therapy.
WS 350.6 F911m]
RJ506.H9F75   1992
618.92'8589—dc20
DNLM/DLC
for Library of Congress   92-9642
                                                              CIP

pro·ed

8700 Shoal Creek Boulevard
Austin, Texas 78757

    4   5   6   7   8   9   10   98   97   96   95

Contents

Acknowledgments

We would like to express our appreciation to a number of people with whom we discussed the concept of this book and to several who read drafts of the manuscript and offered valuable advice and criticism. Our colleagues on the medical staff of the Department of Pediatrics at St. John Hospital in Detroit have been a source of stimulation and continuing education for us. We appreciate the support of administrators and the professional staff of the Evergreen Division of Michigan Health Care Corporation for providing us with a professionally and intellectually stimulating atmosphere within which to work. Psychiatrists Linda Hryhorczuk and Janice Bow read portions of this manuscript and gave us the benefit of their considerable experience. Other professionals and parents who read the first edition and offered comments and advice were immensely helpful, reminding us that our efforts had value to the extent that we offered something useful to our patients and their families.

Introduction

This book has developed from our professional experience with a large number of children with attention deficit–hyperactivity disorder (ADHD). Over the years we have come to understand the frustration and anguish experienced by children with ADHD and by those who live with or teach them. Again and again we have been impressed with the sincerity of parents and teachers who desperately want to help children but are repeatedly frustrated in their efforts by the chronic nature of ADHD.

We have been moved by the sorrow we often see in the faces of children with ADHD who, unable to control their behavior and bewildered by their inability to please their parents, teachers, and peers, are frightened and angry over circumstances they cannot deal with by themselves.

At other times we have observed remarkable gains in many families with all members of the family getting along harmoniously for a time. Then, although things have been going well, the family experiences further troubles when a child reaches a different age and has new expectations and experiences thrust upon him or encounters new sources of stress as he matures and widens his experiences. These plateaus, peaks, and valleys cause a distressing emotional roller coaster ride for everyone.

Although the symptoms of ADHD include the most common behavioral problems in children, we are alarmed by the misinformation and half-truths written about ADHD. Medical and psychological research has produced vast amounts of information, but this information is generally not available to parents and educators. In this book we have combined the most current medical and psychological research findings with our clinical experience gained from nearly 20 years' work with children with ADHD and their families. We have presented the information in this book in a way we hope will be useful to you as you care for your child with ADHD. We suggest that you share this book with others in your child's life.

What Is Attention Deficit–
Hyperactivity Disorder?

Attention deficit–hyperactivity disorder (ADHD) is a syndrome, a cluster of symptoms that includes short attention span, difficulty concentrating, poor impulse control, distractibility, moods that change quickly, and, in some cases, hyperactivity. Children who are overactive, impulsive, or highly distractible are often more difficult to manage or teach than their less active peers. As a result, they are more likely to develop behavior problems.

Attention deficit–hyperactivity disorder is a relatively new term. In the past, children who had one or more of the symptoms of ADHD were often labeled hyperactive or were said to have an attention deficit disorder with hyperactivity or an attention deficit disorder without hyperactivity. There have been many labels used to describe the disorder we now call ADHD and this has created confusion for educators and parents.

Children may have different combinations of the symptoms that make up the syndrome of ADHD. For some children the most obvious symptom is hyperactivity. Another child may not be overactive, but may be very impulsive or inattentive. In fact, there are thousands of different combinations of the symptoms that make up the disorder. They may all be referred to as attention deficit–hyperactivity disorder. Later in this chapter we will present the full technical definition of ADHD.

1

Along with overactivity, difficulty paying attention, and problems with impulsivity and moodiness, children with ADHD also frequently have learning disabilities or emotional problems. Behavioral problems may arise because parents, teachers, and other students find the child's overactivity or impulsivity troublesome. Behavioral and family difficulties may also result from the frustration, anger, and misunderstanding that are so frequently associated with the symptoms of ADHD.

Experts counsel parents to be firm and consistent in the way they manage all their children. This is excellent advice, but what of the child with ADHD who is inconsistent herself? Her behavior may be unpredictable or so unresponsive to attempts to control it that her parents find it impossible to be consistent. In our clinic we frequently hear parents say, "We've tried everything. Some techniques of discipline seem to work for a while, but then they stop working. Now we don't know what to do. He seems to fight everything."

THE PURPOSE OF THIS BOOK

Our concern about the management of children with ADHD arises because we want to make life more pleasant now while the children are young, but also because we are concerned about later adjustment to school, work, and marriage. The past 20 years have yielded a considerable body of psychological and medical research that is a rich source of information for those looking for guidance about how to teach or rear children with ADHD. We have combined our clinical experience with the information available from current medical and psychological research to write this book.

We will begin with definitions and statistics. We do not want to burden you with unnecessary technical information or statistics, but some background is necessary, especially because the day-to-day behavior of children with ADHD can be so puzzling and misleading. We often hear parents and teachers say: "He just doesn't seem to care." "She has the wrong attitude." "She has to have it her way or not at all." "If only he'd stop to think before he does something."

Each of these comments reflects one or more of the symptoms of ADHD, so the place to start is with a clear understanding of the behaviors and personality characteristics under discussion. We will follow definitions and statistics with a careful review of medical, psychological, and educational management programs.

DEFINITION

The diagnostic criteria for ADHD have been established by the American Psychiatric Association. Such a child is inattentive, impulsive, and often hyperactive. The symptoms are sometimes worse in situations where the child must work on her own, such as in the classroom, and the symptoms are not always present.

A diagnosis of ADHD is made when a child has at least 8 of the following 14 symptoms and the disturbance has been present for at least six months:

1. Often fidgets with hands or feet or squirms in seat

2. Has difficulty remaining seated when required to do so

3. Is easily distracted by extraneous stimuli

4. Has difficulty waiting his turn in games or group situations

5. Often blurts out answers to questions before they have been completed

6. Has difficulty following through on instructions from others

7. Has difficulty sustaining attention in tasks or play activities

8. Often shifts from one uncompleted activity to another

9. Has difficulty playing quietly

10. Often talks excessively

11. Often interrupts or intrudes on others

12. Often does not seem to be listening

13. Often loses things necessary for tasks or activities at school or at home

14. Often engages in physically dangerous activities without considering the possible consequences

Research in our clinic by Dr. William Irving showed that half of 150 children diagnosed with ADHD were not hyperactive.

Many children with ADHD are also emotionally labile—their moods change abruptly. Parents comment on how quickly their child's mood changes, not just from good to bad, but back to good again. So, in addition to having behavioral difficulties, children with ADHD often seem more sensitive and easily upset. In some households this causes a constant level of tension as all family members are ever mindful that there could be an emotional outburst at any moment.

The number of children who have ADHD is difficult to determine, partly because different definitions have been used in the past to decide who has the disorder. In general it is agreed that the disorder is common and that, in the United States, it probably occurs in about 3% of all children. ADHD is four to six times more common in boys than in girls. Although it is not inherited directly, the disorder does seem to be more common in some families than others. Because of the preponderance of males with ADHD, most case studies in this book will be of boys. Nonetheless there are many girls with the disorder, and any example of male behavior used for illustration can be applied equally to females.

Two of the best studies on the incidence of ADHD have been published within the past several years. As part of a larger survey of health problems, researchers count the number of children taking medication for ADHD in the Baltimore, Maryland, public schools every few years. In 1987 they found that 5.96% of all public school children were being treated for ADHD. And the number keeps going up. In the 20 years during which this research has been going on, the number of children treated for ADHD in Baltimore has doubled every 5 to 7 years.

Also in 1987, another team of scientists surveyed the school population in the province of Ontario, Canada. Their findings were almost identical to those of the Baltimore study. The Canadian research workers found that exactly 6% of the children in their survey met the criteria for diagnosis of ADHD. The figures included 9% of the boys and 3% of the girls. This figure of three boys to one girl is a lower ratio than earlier studies reported, but it reflects a pattern showing that as survey methods become more accurate and the prevalence of children diagnosed with ADHD climbs to 5% or 6%, the ratio of boys to girls goes down. This most likely indicates that the number of girls is higher than we originally thoughtbut that they are less often diagnosed, in part because they are less likely to cause a disruption in the classroom or at home. Even if they do disturb others they are likely to be labeled emotionally disturbed rather than recognized as having ADHD.

SECONDARY SYMPTOMS

The life of a child with ADHD is not easy. By the time he is 5 years old and begins school, he probably has been criticized, corrected, and even rejected far more than an average child his age. When he begins school, the problems follow him. Teachers may be critical of his inability to sit still and learn a lesson. In many instances, the youngster with ADHD learns that he is not progressing as fast as his classmates, and his self-esteem suffers.

Realizing that he has already been criticized more often than other children, knowing that disaster seems to follow him (more lamps break when he is in the room, more milk is spilled when he is at the table, more furniture is destroyed—and faster—when he is on the scene, and more children seem to wind up pushed down, poked, scratched, or bitten when he is in the group), the frustrations and failures of school don't come as a surprise. Often they serve to confirm for the child with ADHD that he is bad, or stupid, or unacceptable in some other way. Individual children handle this in different ways, but it is common for them to become obstinate, occasionally negative, and often bossy or bullying. They may show low frustration tolerance and frequent outbursts because life is harder for them and more difficult for them to understand. Self-esteem suffers, and after a while it seems as if they don't respond to parents' efforts at discipline.

Consider for the moment how perplexing this must be to the 5- or 6-year-old child with ADHD. Remember your own confusion and frustration and even anger as you tried to understand why your child was so difficult to manage and why she persisted in doing things that only seemed to lead to trouble. This comment from one mother conveys the feelings well. "He just pushes and pushes you until you want to . . . well, I hate to say it, but sometimes I just don't think I can stand it any longer." Well, if from your adult point of view you have been frustrated, confused, and angry, imagine what it must be like for your child. He hears from parents, teachers, brothers and sisters, and neighborhood children a constant chorus reminding him that he is doing things wrong and is upsetting them, but he is unable to step back and understand and then control his own behavior in a way that enables him to satisfy other people and make them happy with his behavior.

From this point of view, it isn't surprising that many youngsters with ADHD develop a second level of emotional and behavioral problems that can be traced back partly to the symptoms associated with the ADHD, but that also are a result of the difficult and unpleasant experiences such youngsters encounter. Failure to understand how these two levels of problems go together is a cause of some of the difficulties and misunderstandings that parents and teachers have when trying to deal with children with ADHD.

EFFECT ON PARENTS AND FAMILIES

Children with ADHD can have a devastating effect on their families. Besides the obvious difficulty in raising a child who is more active, is into more things, and needs more supervision, there are other subtle ways by which children with ADHD disrupt the quality of life. Mothers usually have the day-to-day responsibilities for care, particularly when children are young. As a consequence, it is the mother who feels the greatest burden and the greatest frustration when there are problems. In the early years before the youngster's ADHD is properly diagnosed, this frustration may result in conflict between husband and wife. Many fathers, because their tolerance for certain kinds of aggressive behavior is greater and because they don't see it on a constant basis as the child's mother does, think their child is merely normally active.

It is common to have other family members say the same thing and imply that the only reason the child is more difficult to manage is because of some inadequacy or failing on the part of the mother. Now the mother has three problems to deal with: an overactive child; frustration and anger because of the failure of other people, particularly her husband, to understand and to help; and finally, the beginnings of doubt about her own adequacy as a mother. It is a short step from this point to wondering what she did wrong. She may begin to doubt her common sense and lose faith in her own judgment. Feeling guilty is a natural result.

This combination of unpleasant feelings and attitudes often creates marital problems. The wife comes to feel increasingly misunderstood and overwhelmed with the responsibility of her child. The husband becomes angry with his wife because it seems that he can manage his child so much better than she can. It must be her fault, he concludes. And, because he is usually firmer, has a deeper voice, and has less contact with the child, it is not uncommon to see a child respond more quickly and consistently to a father's directions. A less dramatic version of this same pattern occurs in almost all families.

It would be an error to conclude from this that the mother is the cause of the problem. When a father spends a long time with his child, it quickly becomes clear that many of these frustrating patterns become established as with the mother. With the increased strain in the marriage and the father's dissatisfaction with the way his wife and children are behaving, many fathers tend to pull back. For some this may mean finding excuses to come home for supper a bit later. In those cases where fathers don't go this far, they may subtly withdraw and cut down on the amount of time they spend with their wife or child. This may be illustrated by the father who watches TV, reads a book, retires to a basement workshop, or escapes into a heavy work schedule, shutting out all that is going on around him. The effect is to drive a deeper wedge between husband and wife, weaken further the relationship of father and child, and, finally, greatly contribute to feelings on the part of both parents that they are fighting a battle against a mysterious enemy they cannot fully understand or identify.

One of our colleagues, Dr. Michael McMillan, interviewed couples prior to the birth of their first child and measured the degree of marital satisfaction. A number of months after each child was born Dr. McMillan interviewed the couples again. He found a strong relationship between how the child behaved and marital satisfaction. Easy-to-manage, happy babies caused an increase in satisfaction with the marriage, but very difficult children caused men and women to report substantial increases in dissatisfaction.

WHAT CAUSES ATTENTION DEFICIT–HYPERACTIVITY DISORDER?

There are many unanswered questions about the cause of ADHD, but research has given us some useful information. Children are probably born with the disorder, although in many cases when the child's early development is reconstructed, it is clear that symptoms may not be present from birth. While one mother may claim that her hyperactive youngster was more active even during her pregnancy, another may report that her child enjoyed unremarkable development until 3 years of age, at which time the symptoms appeared. Appearance of symptoms when a child is 2 or 3 years old should not be taken to indicate that the disorder was not present earlier. It is likely that it existed from the beginning of the child's life, and it is only the symptoms that were delayed in making their appearance.

ADHD is not directly inherited, but there is a tendency for the problem to run in families and to be associated with other problems of impulse control. For example, in one study 59 hyperactive children were compared to 41 children who were not hyperactive. The researchers found that 12 parents of the 59 hyperactive children were retrospectively diagnosed as hyperactive based on descriptions of behavior and old school records. However, only two parents of normal children were regarded as possibly having been hyperactive. These statistics illustrate that while not every hyperactive parent produces a child who is hyperactive, there is a greater incidence of hyperactivity in some families than in the population in general.

The tendency for ADHD to run in families suggests that there might be a genetic basis for the problem, at least in some cases. On the other hand, children can learn habits that mimic the symptoms of ADHD by living in the same household with another child or a parent who displays the symptoms. An experienced professional can usually distinguish between a learned pattern of behavior and a true case of ADHD.

The most compelling scientific evidence illustrating the physical basis of the symptoms of ADHD was published in 1990 by Dr. Alan Zametkin, a psychiatrist working in the brain imaging section of the National Institutes of Mental Health, and his co-workers. Since the middle of the 1980s, Zametkin's team has been collecting data from adults who had been diagnosed as hyperactive as children and who still displayed some of the symptoms of what was called hyperactivity when these people were children, but is now referred to as attention deficit–hyperactivity disorder.

The research team used positron emission tomography (PET) to study the metabolism of portions of the patients' brains. To use the PET scan, doctors inject glucose that has been "tagged" with a radioactive chemical into the patients' veins. Glucose is the basic fuel of human cells, so when it is taken up by the cells of the brain, the PET scanner can measure the rate of metabolism by determining how much glucose is used by the brain in a certain period of time.

Comparing the metabolism of hyperactive and normal patients, Zametkin's research team found that in certain areas of the human brain cortex the rate of metabolism, or chemical activity, was significantly slower in hyperactive adults than in normal control subjects.

The research workers mapped the areas of the brain that were most affected. Although this is only preliminary information and much research remains to be done, they found a relationship between the areas of the brain that were affected in the hyperactive subjects and the nature of the symptoms of hyperactivity. For example, areas in the premotor strip that helps control purposeful movements were affected, as were areas in the frontal lobes known to be involved in impulse control.

When these hyperactive adults were treated with medication such as Ritalin®, the chemical activity in the affected areas of their brains was close to that of the normal subjects.

Many questions remain unanswered. What is the nature of the chemical reactions? What chemicals are at the basis of this finding? What causes it? What can be done to prevent it? The answers will take years, but the realization that there is clearly a physical basis for hyperactivity, at least in some cases, should go a long way toward relieving children and adults of the responsibility and blame for the symptoms of ADHD that cause so much anger and diminished self-esteem.

Considering our current knowledge, ADHD should be regarded as a condition that has a physical basis, although neither the cause nor the precise mechanism that causes the symptoms is understood. Most scientists believe that when we finally sort out the answers to our questions, what we now think of as a single ailment will prove to be a number of discrete disorders that might even have different causes and different types of treatment.

HOW IS ATTENTION DEFICIT–HYPERACTIVITY DISORDER DIAGNOSED?

A major problem in diagnosing ADHD is that parents and especially teachers, who are in the best position to observe the symptoms of a young child, do not readily think of ADHD. We must know what we are looking for. We must be alert to the day-to-day, ordinary behaviors that are symptoms of ADHD if we hope to diagnose it as early as possible. We have to have a high "index of suspicion" for a particular problem or diagnosis to have it pop into our minds when we see certain behavior patterns.

There is a saying among physicians: "When you hear hoofbeats you don't think of zebras." This odd expression is intended to remind doctors when they hear or see any sign or symptom to keep in mind not only the most obvious or most likely causes, but every possible cause, including those that are less likely to be involved. Only by considering every possible cause of the symptoms can the physician be sure to make a proper diagnosis.

ADHD is not a rare phenomenon, but it would be good if everyone kept this saying in mind. Symptoms of learning and behavior problems can be misleading. If a medical and psychological evaluation of a child is not sufficiently thorough, or if it is done by someone unfamiliar with commonly occurring physical and psychological disorders, then it is likely that some children will be diagnosed incorrectly. The "zebra's hoofbeats" most often ignored or misunderstood by educators are the symptoms of ADHD.

You already know the technical definition of ADHD, but what behavior do we see in the course of a normal day? Short attention span, distractibility, and problems with impulse control have a direct effect on a child's behavior in the classroom and acquisition of academic skills. For example, it is common to see a child in first or second grade who does not complete her work. Careful observation reveals that the child can and will do the work if someone stands over her and supervises on a one-to-one basis. Because a child works well one-to-one and clearly can learn, it is easy to conclude that the child can do it if she wants to. This seemingly innocent conclusion can be the first step toward a destructive and hurtful process that causes considerable harm for the child and the family.

While there are many possible explanations why a child may not complete schoolwork, it is rarely recognized by educators that ADHD is one of the most common of these. Too often, such a youngster is viewed as either unmotivated or immature, or as lacking a good attitude toward school. It is not uncommon to hear such behavior described as "attention seeking," based on the fact that the child does so well when you give him attention. This is usually a misunderstanding of the circumstances. The reason the child does well when he is given attention is because the parent and/or the teacher organize things for him and use their own longer attention span and ability to focus on materials to keep the child oriented to the task.

Failure to complete schoolwork, then, is one of the zebra's hoofbeats. It should sound an alarm. It should raise your index of suspicion and cause you to ask whether the child may possibly have ADHD.

Similarly, the 5- or 6-year-old child with "motor mouth" or the youngster who always gets in trouble while standing in line may be presenting signs of ADHD. A child who seems unable to wait her turn and blurts out answers in class without raising her hand may be demonstrating symptoms of poor impulse control.

These too are zebra's hoofbeats that should alert parents and teachers to the possible presence of ADHD. Such behavior, if misunderstood or dismissed as immaturity, may be the foundation for later learning and psychological problems.

We want to caution the reader in one important regard. This is a book about attention deficit–hyperactivity disorder. There are other problems that may cause the symptoms described here. For example, anxiety, conduct disorders, and some developmental delays have symptoms that are similar to those of ADHD. Not every child who fails to complete an assignment or talks out of turn has ADHD. Our concern arises from the fact that failure to consider ADHD as one possible cause of these behaviors leads to many cases of ADHD going undiagnosed. A diagnosis of ADHD can only be made by a physician or psychologist who specializes in work with children and is knowledgeable about all of the possible causes of these behaviors.

The criteria used to decide whether a child has ADHD have been described above. Let us consider how they are actually applied. There are no specific tests for ADHD. Rating scales or checklists may help teachers describe the behavior of children, but these tests do not tell whether a child is hyperactive or has ADHD.

For example, we can rate a child's squirminess as he sits at the dinner table or in the classroom. Many hyperactive youngsters are quite fidgety. So are children with other sorts of problems. Anxiety is a common cause of overactivity. Nervous children may display symptoms identical to those of a child with ADHD. They may move about restlessly or, distracted by some troubling matter at home or with friends, may not pay attention to the lesson in school. It is not possible to make a diagnosis of ADHD solely on the basis of even a very careful description of behavior.

Similarly, there are no medical tests such as blood tests or electroencephalograms that allow us to make this diagnosis with certainty. Physicians and psychologists must use several sources of information, combined with their professional experience, to yield a decision about whether a child has ADHD.

History

A child's history is the most important source of information. Although it amuses many observers, mothers of hyperactive youngsters often say that they knew their child was more active while they were still carrying him. "I think my ribs were bruised from the inside," one mother said.

The history of most children with ADHD is not crystal clear. But careful questioning by a professional and equally careful thought and reconstruction of a child's early years by the mother and father will yield important information about the child's activity level and early temperament patterns.

We try to determine whether a child was squirmy as an infant, or possibly more colicky or irritable. A common feature in the early history of youngsters later determined to have ADHD is the report: "She didn't adjust to new circumstances very well." For instance, when changes in feeding were begun or attempts were made to change babysitters or sleep habits, the child found it difficult to get used to the new routines.

As the child got older, it is important to assess how well he was able to pay attention compared to other children. Did he sit quietly and listen to a story when he was 3 years old? How long could she sit and go through a picture book with her mother? Did he watch television programs all the way through? Did she sit through meals? There are long lists of such questions you can probably develop yourself to describe how impulsive, active, and attentive your children have been.

Inborn Temperament Characteristics

No two children are born with exactly the same behavioral characteristics. Just as there are both dramatic and subtle differences in the physical appearance of children, even those born to the same mother and father, there are comparable differences in temperament, personality characteristics, and behavioral style.

Any attempt to diagnose ADHD in a child must include a careful reconstruction of the child's early temperament pattern. An effort must also be made to determine whether the problematic behavior reflects ADHD, is the expression of temperament characteristics, or is a combination of both.

Parents and child-care professionals have long known that there are striking differences in temperament among young children. The systematic study of newborn behavior and its contribution to child development began with the work of a pediatrician and two child psychiatrists, Alexander Thomas, Stella Chess, and Herbert Birch, whose research began in the late 1950s. Although the first reports were published a decade later, only in the past 10 years have pediatricians and psychologists begun to systematically apply the results of these studies to child care and parent counseling.

Child-care professionals are now able to identify nine inborn behavior patterns called *temperament characteristics;* these are based on meticulous observation and descriptions of children's behavior, supplemented with research and clinical experience built on the foundation of this pioneering research. These temperament characteristics provide a good picture of the biological basis of a child's behavior.

The temperament of all children can be described and measured. This fact takes on special significance in the case of children with ADHD, because we have more tools with which to make our observations and attempt to understand the significance of a child's behavior. With this understanding about temperament, children's behavior makes more sense to parents and professionals. This deeper understanding also provides greater precision in child rearing, teaching, and behavior management counseling.

1. *Activity level* refers to the tempo and frequency of movements. A very active child may run, kick, squirm, or crawl all over the house. A child with a low activity level does not usually kick and fuss, lies quietly in the bath, or, in the morning, is still lying in the same place where she fell asleep. These are extremes; most children fall somewhere in between.

2. *Rhythmicity* reflects the degree of regularity of biological functions such as sleeping and waking, rest and activity, and eating and elimination cycles.

3. *Approach and withdrawal* describes a child's reaction when encountering something new, such as food, toys, people, places, or procedures. Some parents describe children who cry when they see a stranger; their preponderant style is to withdraw. Other parents describe their children with comments such as, "She always smiles at a stranger, " or "If he sees a new toy, he goes straight for it." The last two are approach reactions.

4. *Adaptability* is related to approach or withdrawal, which refer to the initial response a child makes. Adaptability deals with the ease with which the initial pattern is changed. The child who spat out cereal when it was first fed to him, but later came to accept it with little fuss, is considered adaptable, while the child who continues to reject food displays nonadaptive behavior.

5. Whether a behavior is positive or negative, it can appear with a high or low *intensity.*

6. *Threshold of responsiveness* refers to the stimulus intensity required to elicit a response from a child. Thresholds may differ for different sensory systems. A child can have a high threshold for visual stimulation, but a low auditory threshold. Some children appear to be very sensitive to any sort of stimulation, while others are best characterized by the statement one mother used to describe her child: "A bomb could go off in his room and he wouldn't bat an eye."

7. *Quality of mood* differentiates between a child whose mood is friendly and pleasant and one who tends to behave in a generally unfriendly or unpleasant manner.

8. *Distractibility* indicates the ease with which behavior can be interrupted by noise or sounds that occur around the child or by the distractions provided by the activity of other people.

9. The last temperament category reflects the child's *attention span and persistence.* Attention span refers to the length of time an activity is pursued; persistence relates to whether an activity is maintained despite distraction and other obstacles. A child can be both highly distractible and highly persistent. Such a child will return to a task again and again, no matter how often she is distracted or diverted.

As might be expected, few children fall at the extremes. If a child's behavior reflects problems at the extreme limits of only one or two categories, he will not be especially difficult to manage.

However, the behavioral style of some children may be marked by irregularity, nonadaptability, withdrawal, and predominately negative moods of high intensity. Not surprisingly, research workers and clinicians choose to call such children "difficult." As infants, difficult children often wake at unpredictable intervals and seem to require less sleep than the average child. Since difficult children do not develop regular sleep cycles as quickly as others, their parents are awakened several times a night and, no matter what technique they may try, they find it frustrating to get these children to sleep at night. Similar unpredictability occurs in the way hunger is expressed. This may be true of elimination cycles as well, and toilet training seems much more difficult. Such children often fret when bathed, cry whenever a new food is introduced, and fuss when a new person enters the room. Leaving the house may result in crying, protesting, and clinging, and the same behavior may occur when the family returns home. The predominance of high-intensity negative moods is shown by relatively more crying than laughing and more fussing than expressions of pleasure.

Most parents will never have children with this clear-cut difficult-child temperament pattern; however, many children will display some of the features. Not all children with difficult temperaments develop serious behavioral or psychological problems. Nonetheless, such children are more difficult to rear, and much depends on the particular combination of child personality characteristics and parent temperament patterns. The history of each child must be carefully evaluated to determine whether a difficult temperament is the primary problem or if it coexists with ADHD.

Tests

The evaluation of a child suspected of having ADHD usually includes a battery of psychological and educational tests. While tests do not lead directly to the diagnosis, they are useful in clarifying certain aspects of a child's behavior. Test scores also provide measurements that can be used later for comparison to assess the effectiveness of treatment.

An *intelligence test* is an important part of the psychological evaluation. An IQ test is used because a child with suspected ADHD often has learning problems. We must determine if the learning problems reflect limited intellectual ability. The most commonly used intelligence test, the *Wechsler Intelligence Scale for Children–Revised,* consists of 10 different subtests, each of which gives the psychologist some specialized information. For example, there are several subtests that measure short-term memory and concentration. Lower scores in these areas of the test provide additional information to be used in deciding whether a child has an attention problem.

Other commonly used tests of intelligence include the *Stanford-Binet Intelligence Scale,* the *Bayley Test of Mental Development,* the *Peabody Picture Vocabulary Test,* and the *Kaufman Assessment Battery for Children.*

Educational tests are designed to measure a child's achievement in reading, spelling, arithmetic, and other academic areas. These tests allow the psychologist to determine the child's achievement level under the best circumstances. Classroom grades often reflect more information than just how much the child has learned. Study habits, incomplete papers, poor preparation for tests, or troublesome behavior in the classroom may all be reflected in a child's grades. Educational tests are necessary in order to determine how much of a handicap the ADHD might be and what areas are being affected.

Among the most commonly used educational tests are the *Wide Range Achievement Test,* the *Woodcock-Johnson Achievement Test,* the *Stanford Diagnostic Reading and Math Tests,* the *Test of Written Expression,* and the *Kaufman Test of Educational Achievement.*

There are two types of *personality tests.* Objective personality tests have clear-cut questions and answers. The *Personality Inventory for Children,* the *Child Behavior Checklist,* and the *Minnesota Multiphasic Personality Inventory* are objective personality tests often used in the assessment of children and their families.

Projective personality tests are less clear-cut in what they require a person to do. The *Sentence Completion Test,* for example, presents the child or adult with a series of partial sentences that can be completed with any idea the respondent chooses. In this case, although the first few words of the sentence are clear, the person can respond in a variety of ways. The psychologist analyzes the content and pattern of the sentences written.

The *Rorschach Inkblot Test* is another example of a projective test. Here it is not only the individual's answers that may come from a variety of thoughts or ideas, but even the nature of the test item itself, the inkblot, is ambiguous. Personality tests of this sort are helpful because they enable a psychologist to gain additional insight into a person's thoughts and feelings and to determine whether other psychological factors exist in addition to, or instead of, ADHD. However, many psychologists question the validity of this test.

Other examples of projective personality tests include the *Thematic Apperception Test* and *Family Drawings.*

A variety of *other specialized tests* may be included in the assessment of a child or an adult. Among the most common are those referred to as perceptual tests. The *Bender Visual Motor Gestalt Test* and the *Beery Developmental Test of Visual Motor Integration* are the most common. Related tests include the *Visual Aural Digit Span Test* and the *Matching Familiar Figures Test.*

The *Gordon Diagnostic System* (*GDS*) is a good example of recent efforts directed toward developing objective measures of attention span and distractibility. The *GDS* consists of a continuous performance or vigilance test during which numbers are presented on a display screen. There are several types of tasks, but the most common one requires a child to press a button whenever a number appears followed by another number, for example, 1 followed by 9.

Sometimes a 9 will appear but not following a 1, and sometimes 1 will flash on the screen but not be followed by 9. This requires that the child pay continuous attention and inhibit impulsive moves. She would make an error if she missed one of the sequences of 1 followed by 9, but she would also make an error if she pushed the button impulsively.

The *GDS* measures impulse control, distractibility, and concentration. It does not directly determine whether a child has ADHD. Errors of omission or commission may occur for many reasons other than ADHD, but the *GDS* is a useful device as part of the evaluation of a child thought to have ADHD. The test also appears to be sensitive to stimulant drug effects.

Rating Scales

A decision about whether a child has ADHD is not difficult to make in extreme cases. But when children are only moderately overactive or inattentive we may have difficulty determining whether this represents a true case of ADHD or whether a youngster's motor just runs a little bit faster than that of an average child. So along with the careful history and test data we want additional information about how a child is behaving right now. Parents and teachers provide valuable information in this regard. A parent can give a long-term, careful, historical point of view about the child. A teacher is often in a valuable position to describe a child's current behavior compared to a large number of other children of the same age.

There are a number of rating scales that can be used to organize this information by parents, teachers, and other professionals trying to determine if certain behaviors are severe enough to be regarded as significant problems. The most popular are the Conners' rating scales. Typically, the rating scales consist of anywhere from 10 to 30 short descriptions of behavior such as those in the following list:

1. Fidgets and can't keep still   Always   Sometimes   Rarely   Never

2. Speaks up or calls out in a
   disruptive manner   Always   Sometimes   Rarely   Never

3. Finishes schoolwork   Always   Sometimes   Rarely   Never

4. Follows direction well   Always   Sometimes   Rarely   Never

The rating scale does not make a diagnosis, but it provides a well-organized description of behavior. Along with the history and observations that doctors make in their examining rooms, this rating scale provides information to help make the diagnosis of whether a child has ADHD.

Standardized questionnaires and rating scales are especially useful in evaluating the symptoms of ADHD because opinions about the severity or seriousness of behavior vary from observer to observer, possibly reflecting the observer's tolerance for certain behavior. Also, the child's behavior may be different from one day to the next, so the written questionnaire helps ensure that everyone is reporting on and making comparisons based on the same information. Information on ordering three well-known rating scales is included at the end of the book.

2

Medical Treatment and Management

Three types of drugs are used to treat children with ADHD: *stimulants,*
tranquilizers, and *antidepressants.* Many people are surprised that the
stimulant medications are far more effective in aiding patients with ADHD
than are tranquilizers or other drugs used to calm people. As in any medical matter, your child's physician should be your guide in using medicine
to treat ADHD. The discussion below is intended to familiarize you with
some of the medicines that are used, as well as some of the issues involved
in deciding what medicines to use, what dosage to prescribe, and why the
medicines work the way they do. This discussion is insufficient to use as a
guide for managing a particular child, and it is important for you to realize
that you may risk your child's safety if you try to alter any dose or type of
medicine after reading this material without first discussing it thoroughly
with your child's physician.

TRANQUILIZERS

Some physicians have used tranquilizers to try to control overactivity and problems with impulse control, with generally poor results.
The most commonly used tranquilizer is thioridazine (Mellaril®). Mellaril

is usually used to control extreme agitation and organically based temper tantrums that, at times, have a major aggressive element. Minor tran quilizers, such as Valium® and Librium®, have been used to treat ADHD as have antihistamines such as Benadryl®. While there may be a use for tranquilizers in a few cases, they are generally less effective than the stimulants for treating ADHD.

STIMULANTS

The most commonly used stimulant drugs are methylphenidate (Ritalin®), dextroamphetamine (Dexedrine®), and magnesium pemoline (Cylert®). The use of stimulants has its origin in the use of Benzedrine® in the 1930s, so physicians have had many years' experience using this type of medicine. Approximately 800,000 people in North America are being treated with stimulant medication at the present time.

Although the neurological mechanisms that explain why stimulants help children with ADHD are not completely clear, there are several theories. Stimulants appear to increase the amount or efficiency of chemical messengers in the central nervous system. At one time, it was thought that some problem in a child's central nervous system caused the child to react to stimulant drugs opposite to the way we would expect. Rather than becoming stimulated and more aroused when given a drug like Ritalin, hyperactive children settled down. We now realize that this is not a paradoxical, or opposite, reaction at all. In fact, children without ADHD also concentrate better when given Dexedrine or Ritalin. In the past few years, we have gained a better understanding of how the nervous system works, and several hypotheses have been suggested to explain how the stimulants work. While none of these hypotheses has been proved, the beneficial effect probably occurs in the following way.

To pay attention and concentrate, we must ignore irrelevant activities going on around us. As you read these words, you may be sitting in a noisy house. Perhaps a television set or stereo is playing. There may be background sound from a fan in your furnace or air conditioner. Cars may be passing in the street outside your home. Of course, if it is too noisy, if there are too many distractions, you cannot concentrate. But most people are able to filter out or ignore stimulation in the background in order to concentrate.

We do not do this consciously; we do not make a decision to ignore each of these stimuli. Instead, our nervous system does it automatically. Children with ADHD seem to be less efficient at doing this. They can, of course, concentrate to some extent. They can filter out some of this noise and activity in the background, but they do not do it as well as we would like. This is where the medicine becomes useful.

Why some children have this problem is unclear, but there are probably several reasons. In some cases, genetic factors are prominent, and these difficulties may run in families. Birth problems, such as insufficient oxygen at some point, could contribute to ADHD, as could certain infections. However, in most cases, we do not know the cause. Nonetheless, we see the beneficial effect of medicine. The drug stimulates and improves the efficiency of the part of the brain that acts as the filtering mechanism to screen out these outside stimuli. It stimulates an inefficient system to work more efficiently. When the drug is working well, the child's nervous system reacts normally.

The complete theory is more complex than this brief explanation, but it helps us understand how a drug like Ritalin enables a child to pay attention better, control impulses better, and become less distractible and less hyperactive. As you can see, the drug seems to work by normalizing the functioning of the child's nervous system, rather than by tranquilizing him or interfering with the normal functioning of his body. This is the reason stimulant drugs are preferred over tranquilizers or other medicines whose effect is caused by making a child drowsy or impairing the efficiency of her nervous system and body.

ANTIDEPRESSANTS

Antidepressant drugs have been used with some success to treat ADHD. They are usually used when stimulants have been tried but either are not effective or produce too many side effects. The most commonly used tricyclic antidepressant is imipramine (Tofranil®). Another is desipramine (Norpramin®).

Still another antidepressant, bupropion (Wellbutrin®), has shown some promise of being helpful in treating the symptoms of ADHD in adults. Dr. Paul Wender, a psychiatrist at the University of Utah School of Medicine who has done research on ADHD for the past 15 years, recently reported results of a study assessing the effectiveness of bupropion. Wender found that of 19 adults with ADHD, 14 experienced moderate to marked benefits from the drug.

Antidepressants are not as widely effective as stimulants. We often need a longer time, sometimes as long as 3 to 4 weeks, to see the positive effect of the medication. Another factor that makes antidepressants a second choice in the treatment of ADHD is their possible side effects. In some cases, antidepressants have an effect on the heart. A doctor who chooses to prescribe an antidepressant for the treatment of ADHD will do a series of routine studies, including an electrocardiogram to monitor the patient's heart.

OTHER MEDICATIONS

Physicians are continually looking for different or better medicines with which to treat ADHD. Patients often tell us that they have heard about a new drug to treat ADHD. This information frequently comes from a newspaper or magazine article citing a report in a medical journal about a new drug that has been found to be moderately effective in treating some of the symptoms of ADHD. One study in a medical journal is not enough to substantiate the value of a new treatment. In many cases, after additional research and trials with the medicine, we find it is no more, or even less, effective than treatments we already have.

For example, for several years clinicians thought that anticonvulsant medications, which are usually used to treat epilepsy, might help children with ADHD. We now know that these drugs are not helpful.

From time to time we do find a medication that is helpful for selected patients or in certain circumstances. Clondine (Catapress®) is a drug of this type. Clondine was originally developed as an antihypertensive to lower blood pressure. Although it is not as effective as the psychostimulants and the antidepressants in treating ADHD in most patients, it is used when children have both ADHD and Tourette's syndrome. (We will have more to say about Tourette's syndrome later in this chapter.)

HOW THE DOCTOR DECIDES WHAT DRUG TO USE

There are no absolute guidelines to help a physician know which drug to prescribe. Approximately 75% of children with ADHD respond positively to some extent to one of the stimulants. Some children who respond well to Ritalin do not do well on Dexedrine or Cylert. The opposite is also true. Generally, physicians prescribe the drug with which they have had the most experience and the one they think is best for a child. In some cases it is necessary to change the prescription and try a different medicine. Trying a second or even third medicine is a normal and safe procedure.

Ritalin is the drug most familiar to pediatricians, child psychiatrists, and pediatric neurologists and therefore is prescribed most often. Cylert is the newest of the three stimulants. Ritalin and Dexedrine may be administered in several doses at roughly 4-hour intervals throughout the day or in a single sustained-release, or spansule, form once in the morning. Only one form of Cylert is available, a long-acting dose taken in the morning.

The sustained-release medications have several advantages. They reduce the possibility of error or forgetting a noontime dose. They also save children the social embarrassment of being different from other students. Teenagers are often self-conscious about going to the principal's or nurse's office for medicine at lunchtime. This is one of the reasons teenagers try to avoid taking medicine. Long-acting medication such as Cylert and sustained-release Ritalin and Dexedrine offer a welcome opportunity to avoid embarrassment and conflict. Nonetheless, there are instances when divided doses throughout the day have a better therapeutic effect or are more desirable for other reasons.

Children who respond well to divided doses of Ritalin may not have an equally positive response to the sustained-release form of the medication. Many children do not do as well on sustained-release Ritalin (Ritalin SR®) as on divided doses. This is especially important to keep in mind if your child has been doing well taking medicine in the morning and at lunchtime and, for convenience, your doctor switches to Ritalin SR. Be alert for changes in behavior. If the quality of behavior or schoolwork deteriorates, this may reflect the lessened effectiveness of the medication.

Why some children respond well to divided doses of Ritalin and not to the sustained-release formula is unclear. There is some preliminary evidence to suggest that in some children Ritalin SR is not absorbed evenly from the digestive system throughout the day, and consequently the therapeutic level in the bloodstream varies more than with the divided doses.

The decision whether to administer medicine several times through the day or in a form requiring only a single administration in the morning is something that should be discussed with your child's doctor.

HOW DOES THE DOCTOR DECIDE ON THE DOSE?

Just as choosing a drug is a matter of making an initial careful trial, so is deciding on a proper dose. Most physicians begin a child on a small dose of a stimulant and then wait to see the effect this has on behavior. If necessary, the medicine can be increased in small steps until the desired effect is obtained or until it becomes clear that the medicine is not helping, at which point it is discontinued and another drug is tried. The therapeutic effect may be evident within a few days with Ritalin or Dexedrine and may take longer with Cylert.

Research in the past few years has shown that it is no longer sufficient just to ask what the best dose is for a particular child or a particular purpose. The dose of a stimulant necessary to control a child's hyperactivity may not be the same dose required to best control a problem with paying attention. To complicate this matter even more, a different dose may be required to gain maximum control of the child's impulsivity, and a still different dose for the best effect on emotional changes.

Fortunately, for most people, the doses necessary to control different symptoms are roughly the same. For some children, they are identical. For a number of children, however, we must compromise and make a decision about which symptom we are most concerned about. To get optimum control in one area we may have to sacrifice some control of other symptoms.

Even if it is impossible to obtain perfect control of all symptoms, understanding how the medicine works on different symptoms helps us plan more effectively. For example, consider the child who has a short attention span and is hyperactive. Behavior modification techniques are more effective and easier to implement for hyperactivity than for short attention span. If we cannot get good control of both symptoms with medication, our choice would be to regulate the medicine based on improvement in attention span and completion of schoolwork and use a behavior modification program for the hyperactivity.

Some behavior is easier to measure. For example, if a child is very active it is easy to see if medicine slows him down. On the other hand assessment may be harder for a teacher if a child has only a subtle disturbance in attention span that results in inefficient learning. Progress in attainment of academic skills is not something that can be measured on a day-to-day basis. Consequently, it has been the practice of many physicians to regulate the dose of medicine based on reports of the most observable behavior. Thus, activity level or impulse control problems may be used as a measure of the medicine's effectiveness. The fact that this may not be the optimal dose for learning is neglected. Once the child's behavior is under control, the teacher may find that learning has not progressed at a commensurate rate. Further adjustment of the dose may be necessary, sacrificing some control in behavioral areas to gain better achievement.

USE OF MEDICATION WITH ADOLESCENTS AND ADULTS

It is common practice for many physicians to routinely stop prescribing medication for children with ADHD when they reach a certain age. Although the need for medication and the dosage should be reassessed at intervals, there is now a substantial amount of evidence that stimulants continue to be helpful through the teenage years and into adulthood.

The reason many practitioners discontinue medication when a child is 13 or 14 years old seems to be based on two mistaken notions. First, children were thought to outgrow ADHD when they reach the early stages of puberty. This erroneous conclusion is based on the observation that many children do, indeed, become less active at that time. If the psychologist or physician looks only at activity level, without considering impulse control problems and attention span, the conclusion may be that the problem no longer exists.

The second reason for discontinuing psychostimulants with teenagers and young adults is that, until the last few years, there were no published reports in the adolescent or adult psychiatric journals demonstrating that medication was helpful. That research has now been done, and the publication of several influential articles in *Pediatrics,* the *Journal of Child Psychiatry,* and the *American Journal of Psychiatry* has made practitioners more aware of the value of medication with older individuals.

Decisions to treat older adolescents and adults with medication should be based on the same criteria used to decide to treat younger children. First, the diagnosis has to be made. Then, a determination must be made of the extent to which the symptoms of ADHD interfere with the person's life. For many adults, medication will not be necessary. Simply understanding ADHD in its adult form and recognizing how the symptoms affect day-to-day living, work, and family relationships is often immensely helpful in enabling the adult to accept the symptoms and compensate for them. In some cases medication is appropriate. For example, we have observed the benefits of Ritalin for adults attending school. Some occupations require sustained attention, and often medication enables a person to work with greater efficiency.

In our clinic, about half of the adult patients who are taking medication are on Ritalin and the other half are on antidepressants. Desipramine (Norpramin) is the most commonly used antidepressant in our clinic.

Other adults with ADHD can also benefit from Ritalin. For example, one of our patients was a roofer. In the 2 years prior to his diagnosis and start of treatment for ADHD, he fell off three roofs. Fortunately, his injuries were not life threatening, but he did break several bones. The potential danger for a distractible, inattentive man working in a dangerous occupation is clear. Our roofer has been taking Ritalin for nearly 3 years now and he has not fallen off any roofs during this time.

We cannot overemphasize the value of making a diagnosis of ADHD in an adult. In chapter 4 we will have more to say about the special problems parents with ADHD have in managing children with ADHD. At this point, we want to stress the importance of recognizing that ADHD persists throughout life and that troublesome symptoms for children can be equally troublesome for adults.

OTHER POINTS ABOUT TREATMENT WITH MEDICATION

It is important to administer your child's medicine according to the physician's instructions. Many problems can be traced to poor habits in taking medicine, such as changing the dose frequency or the size of the dose without physician consultation. Your child's doctor might give you some discretion in adjusting the dose of medicine, taking into consideration your reports about your child's behavior. However, without that instruction, you should stick carefully to the prescribed schedule.

Stimulant drugs work differently from many other medicines people know well, such as antibiotics, which are prescribed for a short period of time and usually "cure" the child's illness. Stimulant drugs do not cure children, and continued use of medicine on a regular basis is necessary. Most parents are used to the idea that you either have an illness or you do not. That model of disease is not appropriate when considering ADHD. After a child has been symptom-free for a few weeks or months, some parents get a little sloppy with the medicine. It is as if they say to themselves, "Well, I guess we finally have this under control"; they then forget a dose of the medicine and the behavior problems reappear.

Another misunderstanding is common. Children with ADHD are far more normal than abnormal. As normal children, they have the usual moods and temperament changes that you might expect. Like everyone else, they have good days and bad days, happy days and sad days. There are days when they are irritated and cannot wait to get through the day, and there are days they greet with enthusiasm and joy. When your child has a fight on the playground similar to the fights he had before treatment with medicine, do not assume that the medicine is no longer working properly. Children have fights on the playground and get into other trouble for reasons that have nothing to do with hyperactivity or concentration problems. Do not assume that all the problems that arise reflect either

ADHD or the inadequacy of the medicine. There is no medicine that makes any child perfect.

Approximately 50% of all prescribed medicine is not taken the way it is prescribed. This runs the gamut from never filling the prescription to not taking the medicine in accordance with the doctor's instructions. Because this happens so often, it probably reflects something about human nature that will never change. We should, however, be aware of the problems these habits might lead to when we give medicine to children with ADHD.

HOW DO YOU TELL A CHILD WHY HE'S TAKING MEDICATION?

Children should know why they are taking medicine. Unfortunately, when asked why they take Ritalin, Cylert, or Dexedrine, children often answer, "Because I'm bad," or "It helps me be good." It is possible to explain medicine usage without adding to a child's feelings of inadequacy or making him feel that drugs are a way to control behavior.

It is sufficient to tell most children that they have trouble concentrating and getting their work done. The medicine is useful because it helps them pay attention better and finish their work. This should be an adequate explanation even for the child who has a moderate behavior problem with poor impulse control. Under no circumstances would we ever suggest lying to a child or even taking advantage of her innocence to subtly mislead her.

There is little advantage to be gained by explaining in detail to a young child that the medicine also helps with impulse control and will help keep him out of trouble. He will be quite aware that it is easier to get his work done and will increasingly notice that he gets along better with other people.

A similar explanation about the medication's effect on impulse control or "acting without thinking" is helpful. Combine these experiences in discussions with your child to help her take greater credit for the positive things that are happening. Explain that the medicine is simply a little bit of help to get her started.

ADHD AND DIET

There are two points of view regarding diet and ADHD. The most popular one follows the writings of Benjamin Feingold, a California pediatrician who, in 1974, wrote a book for parents, *Why Your Child Is Hyperactive*. Based on his clinical experience, Feingold recommended that artificial flavors and colors, along with preservatives, refined sugar, and natural salicylate, be removed from a child's diet. He claimed that this helped a large number of children with ADHD.

The other approach to diet is that of the orthomolecular psychiatrists. It is their belief that there is a biochemical balance or insufficiency of naturally needed chemicals in the brains of many people, including children with ADHD and learning disabilities. Large doses of vitamins, most commonly vitamins C, B_3, and B_6, are supposed to cure the problem. Orthomolecular psychiatrists believe that vitamin deficiencies also underlie many serious mental disorders, such as schizophrenia.

There are Feingold societies throughout the United States and Canada and cookbooks have been prepared describing additive-free diets, but there is no scientific evidence that such diets help even a handful of children with ADHD. Nonetheless, because it is such a popular notion, it is worth discussing a bit more fully.

Many parents of children with ADHD have noticed that when their children eat especially large amounts of sweets at Halloween, Christmas, or Easter, their behavior becomes even more uncontrollable. So although there is no scientific proof that refined sugar and artificial substances cause hyperactivity or attention problems, there are so many reports from parents that we cannot ignore them. The observation that large amounts of sweets make children with ADHD worse can easily be misinterpreted. It does not follow that, if you take all the sugar out of your child's diet, you will cure him. It may be that many people are sensitive to large amounts of refined sugar, which caused the problem in the first place. Just because two facts are connected does not mean that you can determine cause and effect; if you have a headache and aspirin works to relieve the pain, it does not prove that you got the headache because your body needed aspirin.

We are satisfied that research and extensive clinical experience have shown that sugar does not cause ADHD. Sugar can, however, make matters worse for some children with ADHD. The relationship between eating sugar and behavioral changes is complex, and the results of the research are contradictory. For example, researchers at one medical center in Pittsburgh reported that no matter how much sugar most children with ADHD ate, it caused no change in their behavior. On the other hand, Keith Conners, who has done extensive work on diet and ADHD over the years and who is the author of the 1980 book *Food Additives and Hyperactive Children*, claims that the effect of sugar on a child's behavior depends on what else the child has recently eaten. Children who have fasted or eaten high-protein diets are not affected no matter what amount of sugar they eat.

Children who have just completed high-carbohydrate meals, however, show a definite reaction to sugar, and the quality of their behavior deteriorates.

There have been a few reports in medical journals of children responding favorably to changes in diet. It has been our practice to inform parents of the current status of medical and psychological opinion in this area and not discourage them if they want to use a Feingold-type diet. The diet is difficult and expensive to implement because many of the necessary foods are not readily available. Although there is no reason to expect it to work, it is not dangerous. In many ways it is as healthy or more so than the diet most people follow. Even if it doesn't help with hyperactivity and attention problems, it is a nutritious way to eat. We try to be very careful to avoid encouraging parents to use the diet, however. It is easy to fail or give up. The best that can be said about additive-free diets is that they are not harmful, but they do not seem to work. However, if you want to give them a try in your house, there is no reason not to.

The same advice cannot be given about orthomolecular treatment because it is necessary to give your child large doses of vitamins. Since vitamin therapy is without any scientific support, there seems little reason to use it, and it should not be attempted without a careful discussion with your child's doctor. Some children do have vitamin deficiencies, and some require large doses of vitamins for other reasons. But we are not aware of any evidence, except for the reports of a few orthomolecular psychiatrists, based on their own experiences, that large doses of vitamins help children with ADHD.

A 5-year collaborative study by the board of directors of the Canadian Mental Health Association strongly suggests no therapeutic effect from vitamin B treatment. Several years ago, the American Psychiatric Association published a report, "Megavitamin and Orthomolecular Therapy in Psychiatry." After reviewing the history and literature relating to this subject, the members of the committee concluded: "In our view, the results and claims of the advocates of megavitamin therapy have not been confirmed by several groups of psychiatrists and psychologists experienced in psychopharmacological research." Thus, the claims the megavitamin proponents made as far back as 1957 have not been confirmed. The committee said, "Under these circumstances, this task force considers the massive publicity which they promulgate using catch phrases which are really misnomers like megavitamin therapy and orthomolecular treatment to be deplorable."

ADHD AND ALLERGIES

Medical reports indicate that there is a higher incidence of allergies in children with ADHD. There does not seem to be a connection between any particular kind of allergy and ADHD, but more children with ADHD have allergies. In fact, this was one observation that led Feingold to suggest that children with ADHD are physiologically more sensitive and need to be more careful about the substances they are exposed to.

The observations that have been made connecting allergies with ADHD do not suggest that one causes the other. They may both be caused by, or connected to, a yet unknown third factor or not connected at all. Knowing this relationship does not, however, give us guidance about any specific therapy. At this time, the importance of the apparent connection between allergies and ADHD lies in the possibility that this information may lead, through further research, to better means of treating both disorders.

Several medicines used by allergists may cause symptoms similar to those of ADHD. Although antihistamines make most children drowsy, they make some children more active. The bronchial dilator theophylline is claimed to have a variety of side effects, including nervousness, restlessness, insomnia, and irritability. In one study, children with mild asthma were divided into two groups. One group received theophylline, the other a placebo. Although parents were unable to note any changes in the children's behavior and there was no evidence on psychological tests that they were affected, teachers were consistently able to tell which children were receiving the drug and which the placebo. The children on the medication were described as more irritable, more active, less able to deal with unstructured time, and easily distracted from work. The results of this study, taken together with several others, offer support for the observation that the side effects of certain commonly used drugs may cause behaviors that mimic the symptoms of ADHD in some children.

Of particular concern is the question of how to medically treat the allergic child who also has ADHD. There have been no studies to show whether youngsters with ADHD are more sensitive to theophylline or other drugs. To our knowledge, there have been no reports to indicate that bronchial dilators cannot be used at the same time as medicines to treat ADHD.

Managing the behavior of an asthmatic child with ADHD can be complex. It is made more difficult by the fact that a pediatric allergist may treat the child's asthma, and a pediatrician or child psychiatrist the ADHD. It is essential that you make clear to your doctor, or both doctors, the nature of your child's symptoms and observe whether the symptoms are made worse by the use of theophylline or other drugs. Do not make any adjustment in the medication yourself. Consult with the doctors and be patient. When a child has both disorders, it often takes time to get a clear-cut picture of the causes of each symptom and to determine the best treatment plan.

MEDICATION AND LATER DRUG USE

Drug use is a serious problem. The question of whether use of long-term medication to help control behavior early in a child's life might lead to later drug abuse is one that must be addressed. Fortunately, the results of several careful experiments following children over a long period of time are very reassuring. So far, no one has found that taking Ritalin or any other drug to control ADHD causes problems with drugs later in life. In fact, two interesting studies by researchers in the Department of Psychiatry at the University of Iowa and at Detroit's Lafayette Clinic suggest that just the opposite is true.

The Iowa research workers studied 51 boys who had been referred to their clinic because of hyperactivity, learning difficulties, and behavior problems. Twenty-six of the boys were given stimulant medication, while 25 received only short-term, behaviorally oriented counseling. The children were between the ages of 6 and 12 when first seen. A follow-up study was done 5 years later, when they were 11 to 17 years old. The researchers were interested in the answers to a number of questions. One of the most important was whether there was a relationship between use of stimulant medication and drug abuse. They found a relationship, but it was opposite to what we might have feared. Unmedicated subjects, those who had not received stimulant medication, were significantly more likely to report that their friends asked them to smoke marijuana, and they were significantly more likely to report that they had tried marijuana. Another finding, although not statistically significant, was that in the previous month more unmedicated subjects had experimented with tranquilizers and had more drinks of alcohol at one time than the children who had been treated with stimulant drugs.

Keep in mind that in this experiment, two groups of children with ADHD were being compared. Nonetheless, the results of the study clearly answer the question of whether using stimulant drugs causes any drug problems later on. In fact, it may be that denying the stimulant medicine to the 25 children who received only behaviorally oriented counseling may have led to greater interpersonal difficulties and more unhappiness for them over the years. This, in turn, might have been related to their drug misuse.

USE OF DRUGS DURING SCHOOL HOLIDAYS AND ON WEEKENDS

As in all questions about the use of medicine, your child's physician should be the final authority for decisions about drug dosage. Here, we will discuss some considerations that go into making decisions about whether a child should continue on medication during school holidays and weekends. The medications we are reviewing here have a very short active life in a child's body. Three or 4 hours after Ritalin is taken the therapeutic effect is gone, although traces of the drug remain in the child's system for a considerable period of time. Though there is some disagreement in this area, it is generally believed that the medicine has little, if any, cumulative effect. This means that a dose of Ritalin at 7:30 on Monday morning is equally effective regardless of whether the child has taken the medicine continuously throughout the weekend. This is, of course, different from the use of many medicines you may be familiar with. If you have an infection and are taking an antibiotic, you must adhere strictly to the schedule of drug administration, or subsequent doses may be less effective. Decisions to continue Ritalin over the weekend or during school holidays usually depend on how the child behaves without the medicine.

There are some children for whom there is an advantage to being given the medicine 7 days a week. We refer here to children whose behavior differs so much when they are off the medicine that they become bewildered or frustrated by the dramatic differences in their behavior. For example, one 10-year-old boy told us, "I can't stand it on the weekend. I know that I should be able to do things and to pay attention and to control my own behavior, but I can't. I can't stand it."

We prefer to help the child recognize the nature of the disorder and learn to live with the problem, but some children are troubled more than others. In cases where the child himself describes his distress in such dramatic terms, consideration ought to be given to administering the medicine throughout the entire week. We are very cautious, of course, about encouraging children to look to medication as a solution for their problems or allowing them to become so dependent on medicine that they lose the motivation to seek ways to deal with their problems themselves. This is a thorny dilemma, but the option of using medication in this way should be kept open.

A commonsense rule with any drug that might be taken for a long period of time is that the fewer pills a child takes, the better, even in the case of relatively safe medication, such as psychostimulants. The simplest rule for deciding whether to use the medicine on the weekend is to see if the family and the child with ADHD can manage without it. If they can, do not use it. Occasionally, it might be necessary to use medicine on the weekend, although not on a regular schedule. For example, your child may need medicine on Sunday morning before church. Or there may be a family gathering Saturday evening that overwhelms the child unless she has had her medicine. This use is often appropriate, but again, we caution you that if you wish to use Ritalin, Cylert, or Dexedrine in this way, you should first discuss it with your physician. The general advice we offer is intended to alert you to the issues involved in order to broaden your understanding of what is happening with your child. Specific medical decisions require your doctor's consultation; he or she knows your child's individual needs.

Many children who take Ritalin regularly during the school year can manage without it during the summer. Other children are better off taking medication in the summer too. Their impulsivity can interfere with the quality of their social relationships, or it may disrupt the family enough to cause severe negative psychological consequences. In other words, it is usually best to try to get by without stimulants during the summer or over long vacations, such as the Christmas holiday. However, if your child cannot manage and his life is a disaster without it, then, of course, the best plan is to continue with the medicine.

WHEN SHOULD YOU ASK THE DOCTOR ABOUT DISCONTINUING MEDICATION?

The decision to stop giving a child stimulant medication is a complex one. A number of factors must be taken into consideration. Most important is the realization that it often is not possible to determine in advance if a child will be able to manage satisfactorily without medication. In most cases, a carefully controlled trial, either on holidays, as we have just discussed, or at other times, is the best way to find out. Since children do not take psychostimulants 24 hours a day, there is usually a drug-free period each day when parents can evaluate the effectiveness of the medicine. This will be more difficult in cases where the child takes medicine only for school and parents have no basis for comparison.

Many people find it hard to stick to a schedule for taking medicine. As previously mentioned, it is estimated that 50% of adult patients do not take medication as prescribed. For children these figures may be worse. Even in cases where children have to take medicine such as antibiotics for as short a time as 10 days, many patients stop their medication early. It was discovered in one study that 56% of patients had stopped taking such medicine by the 3rd day. In another study, researchers found that only 7.3% of 300 pediatric patients completed their course of antibiotics for ear infections.

Many parents change or discontinue medicine without consultation with their physician. This is done because patients do not fully understand what the medicine is supposed to do and why it has to be continued for such a long time. A recent study was conducted at the Children's Hospital of Eastern Ontario in Canada. ADHD patients taking Ritalin were followed over a period of 10 months. Twenty percent of the patients stopped using the medicine by the end of the 4th month. By the end of the 10th month, only 55% of the children were still taking their prescribed medicine. Fewer than 10% of the families consulted their physicians prior to terminating the medication.

It is tempting to discontinue medicine after your child has been taking it for a long time. In some cases there are no immediate changes in the child's behavior or, if there are changes, they occur in school or are covered up by other events in the child's life. Most parents who stop giving their child medicine do not start it again on their own. We regard figures such as these with considerable concern. As we have observed many times, management of children with ADHD is difficult and frustrating. It becomes more complicated and troublesome when decisions about discontinuing medicine are made without careful medical consideration.

Although the most common medication error parents make is to not give medicine consistently, there is another mistake parents and teachers often make together. A teacher may observe a child who has been doing well on medicine gradually seem to resume old habits. It looks as if the medicine is no longer working.

It would be a rare teacher or parent who would ever suggest that a child take medicine that was not prescribed by a physician. It is not, however, unusual for a parent and teacher, deciding together, to stop giving prescribed medicine without consultation with the doctor. In the child's case just mentioned, medication is discontinued to see the effect this has on behavior. If the child does not get worse, the parent and teacher may mistakenly conclude that the medicine was not doing anything, because the child is no worse off having stopped the medicine.

Such an observation might be true, but the conclusion that the medicine was not helping is frequently an error. Children may need increased amounts of medication for several reasons. First, as their bodies grow, they may need a larger dose. Also, some children's bodies get used to certain doses of medicine, so they need a higher dose to continue to benefit. Parents and teachers who think they have done a scientific experiment to evaluate the effectiveness of medicine may have actually been led to a false conclusion. The reason a child's behavior may not deteriorate further when medicine is discontinued is because the medicine was already at too low a level to provide any benefit. Therefore, the fact that the child's behavior shows no change when the medicine is stopped is not a true measure of the medicine's effectiveness.

In most cases, parents do not discuss with the child's doctor the decision to stop giving medicine, or it may be mentioned during the next routine visit to the doctor's office. In our example, the student usually completes the school year without medication. It may not be until the following fall, when the first teacher conferences occur or the first report cards come out, that any alarm is raised about how badly the child is doing. Then, with appropriate medical and psychological follow-up, the child is normally put back on medicine at an adjusted dose, which provides the same benefit that was evident early in the preceding year. Sometimes it takes several years for the child to get back on medicine because the parents think that the medication was ineffective, and they do not bring it up again with their doctor.

There are two simple steps to take when a child who previously responded to medicine no longer seems to benefit from it. First, check and make sure that the child is taking the medicine as prescribed. Second, recognize that medicine's failure to continue to do the job is often an indication that the dose is now too low. The proper experiment for parents to try, if permitted by the doctor, is to give a higher dose to see if it results in an improvement in the child's behavior.

WHEN CHILDREN REFUSE TO TAKE MEDICATION

Reluctance to take medication frequently occurs among teenagers, but at times it is a problem for children as young as 9 or 10. There are three main reasons. Refusal may be a continuation of the battle for control between parents and child. Younger children can often be forced to take their medicine. However, in the case of a teenager whose deteriorated relationship with his parents involves constant battles for supremacy and control, there is little parents can do to force compliance. The greater the effort made to get the child to take medicine, the more resistance is encountered.

The second reason children refuse medication is social pressure. This problem occurs most often when a child must take medication in school, because children do not want to be different. Even if a child is not teased and others do not even know about the medication, the child's self-conscious feelings and fears about what her friends might think are sufficient to make her resist the medication.

The third reason children refuse medication is more subtle and complex. Some children simply say, "I don't need medicine. There's nothing wrong with me." Efforts to talk to the child about the nature of ADHD and the behavior and learning problems it creates are usually met with either an argument or flat denial. A child may say, "I can pay attention if I want to."

In such a case we have to be mindful that the child is not insisting that there is nothing wrong with him because he feels good about himself, or because he doesn't know that his schoolwork is a problem or his behavior is difficult. The child is only too aware that there is something wrong, and he finds the idea so upsetting that he refuses to acknowledge it. Typically, the more he is threatened by the disorder, the more vehement is his insistence that there is nothing wrong with him. Efforts to convince him that he does have a problem usually meet with failure. They only add to the child's distress, make him more anxious, and cause him to erect an even more impenetrable barrier to keep from recognizing the truth.

In most cases, we have found that children take this position only after a number of years during which the ADHD was either undiagnosed or misunderstood. Parents and teachers unintentionally caused the child to view himself as inadequate or a failure. When children deny that they have ADHD, even when it is carefully explained to them, we have to ask why they are running from the truth. The most common reason is that they have been made to feel bad about themselves over the years, through misdiagnosis, misunderstanding, or improper management at home or at school.

Most children can be persuaded to accept medication if we take the time to understand their refusal and deal with the underlying problems first. In the case of a child who is too frightened to acknowledge that there is something wrong with her, this may take quite a bit of time to resolve. Once the child comes to the point where she can accept her limitations and understand why she resists facing the disorder, issues of medical compliance and taking medicine on schedule can be dealt with more easily.

SIDE EFFECTS

Listed below are 17 symptoms that have been mentioned as possible side effects of psychostimulants.

Decreased appetite	Reduction in talking
Insomnia	Anxiety

Abdominal pain	Lack of interest in others
Headaches	Euphoria
Tendency to cry	Irritability
Tics or nervous movements	Nightmares
Dizziness	Sadness
Drowsiness	Staring
Nail biting	

Dr. Russell Barkley and co-workers from the departments of Psychiatry and Pediatrics at the University of Massachusetts Medical Center studied children treated with Ritalin. They found that when side effects did occur, they were usually relatively mild. In cases where more serious side effects occurred, decreasing or discontinuing medication eliminated the side effects. Of 83 children in their study, only 3 had side effects serious enough so that medication had to be stopped. Of the 17 symptoms that have been reported as possible side effects of Ritalin, Barkley and his research team found that only four were directly related to drug use: insomnia, decreased appetite, abdominal pain, and headaches.

Nearly half of the children in the study experienced some insomnia and nearly two-thirds had some loss of appetite while taking the medication. However, this fact has to be balanced against the finding that 40% of the patients complained of loss of appetite and 15% of insomnia while taking a placebo. Suggestion may play a significant role in causing what appear to be side effects. In addition, Barkley interpreted these findings as indicating that many of the behavioral side effects attributed to stimulant medication already occur in a sizable number of children with ADHD.

The most common short-term side effects resulting from the use of stimulants are insomnia, decreased appetite, abdominal pain, and headaches. Side effects such as these occur only in a minority of children and they tend to be minor and temporary. If, however, they are severe or last longer than several days, you should discuss them with your child's physician. Stimulant medication can make some children irritable and whiny. Although this occurs in fewer than 5% of children treated with psychostimulants, the problem can be serious enough to discontinue medication. Normally these side effects are evident immediately; in some cases they do not appear until the dose is increased or until later in treatment.

The decision to continue treating a child with medication in such circumstances is difficult. In many cases there is minimal benefit from the medicine, so the decision to discontinue it is easy. In other cases, the medicine works as it should; the child concentrates better, is less active, and is less impulsive. Nonetheless, the irritability and fussiness may be more than parents can tolerate.

There is a relationship between age and the side effects of irritability and whininess. These symptoms are more common in children younger than 5 years of age. Children who display a variety of side effects, including increased irritability, when they are given the medicine at age 4 or 5 are often able to benefit from the medicine as they get older.

Side effects with one stimulant may not occur with another. It is usually a good idea to try other medications for careful trials before giving up on treatment with medication.

There is only limited information available about the long-term side effects of stimulation. One long-term side effect parents often ask about is possible decrease of growth rate. A number of studies were published in the late 1960s and early 1970s suggesting that long-term use of high doses of stimulants, particularly Dexedrine and Ritalin, slowed children's growth. A recent review of all published literature by a panel of the Food and Drug Administration suggests, however, that any height and weight suppression occurs for only the first year or two of therapy; there does not seem to be any long-term effect on ultimate growth. We have already discussed the question of whether there is a tendency for children treated with stimulants to become drug abusers later in life.

DRUG TOLERANCE

Most children with ADHD respond well to treatment with psychostimulants and other carefully chosen medications. Nonetheless, it is not unusual to find that a patient who has been doing well on medication for a while will take a turn for the worse. We usually do not see a sudden change. Only when parents and teachers look back over several months does it become clear that the problem has been developing for some time.

If a child takes medicine regularly and as prescribed, there are two reasons why it may seem to have stopped working. First, the child may have grown. The bigger child normally requires a larger dose of medication. Growth of even 1 inch or the addition of 5 to 10 pounds may make a certain dosage inadequate to control the symptoms of ADHD. This does not mean that the problem has worsened. In fact, the actual relationship between body size and the number of milligrams of medication may not have changed at all.

The second reason why medicine may not work is because of the development of a tolerance to the drug. A dose that used to work well no longer is adequate to control behavior. Usually, increasing the size of the dose brings the behavior back under control but, for a few people, improvement may last only a short period of time and then a still larger dose becomes necessary.

A patient who has developed a drug intolerance requires consistently increased doses of medication to maintain control over the symptoms of a medical problem. Individuals vary in the extent to which they develop a tolerance or whether they develop a tolerance at all.

For some patients with ADHD, the development of a tolerance to one or more of the psychostimulants can create considerable complications in medical management of the disorder. Fortunately, only moderate increases in dosage are necessary for most patients and a long time passes before tolerance develops again. For a few patients, however, tolerance develops more quickly; they may require dosages near the upper limits of what is considered safe. In such cases, the physician may substitute another drug for a while.

For example, a patient who has developed a tolerance to Ritalin might be treated for several months with Cylert or Dexedrine. One drug probably works best, so after a time on an alternate medication the child's doctor usually returns to the original medicine, often at a lower dose because tolerance has diminished again.

The development of tolerance is one reason many physicians recommend drug holidays as often as possible. Most patients do not develop a tolerance to any of the psychostimulants, and if a child does not take medication on weekends, school holidays, or in the summer, he is less likely to develop such a tolerance. In fact, children whose medication is at a higher level by the end of the school year may return to school in September after a drug-free summer at the same or a lower dose with equal effectiveness.

Unless there is a serious problem in regulating your child's medication because of the development of a drug tolerance, we do not recommend that concern about tolerance should be the primary basis for decisions about whether to give your son or daughter medication on weekends or school holidays. We believe that the control of ADHD symptoms, the quality of the child's life, and the quality of family life are the primary determinants. If your child's behavior causes problems in peer or family relationships during school holidays to the point where the family's quality of life is considerably diminished or the child's self-esteem continues to suffer, a decision to continue medication is best made on the basis of those observations. Concern about developing a drug tolerance is only one factor to be taken into consideration.

TICS AND TOURETTE'S SYNDROME

A tic is a sudden, involuntary, repetitive, purposeless, stereotyped movement. Some tics are simple and involve a limited group of muscles. Nodding the head and blinking the eyes are examples of simple tics. Other tics reflect more complicated movements. Chronic tic disorders have been subdivided according to whether they only consist of motor tics or include both motor and vocal tics. The latter are referred to as *Tourette's syndrome.*

We include a discussion of tics and Tourette's syndrome here because occasionally tics are difficult to distinguish from the symptoms of ADHD. Furthermore, some older reports in medical journals suggested that treatment of children with psychostimulants may cause tics or Tourette's syndrome as a side effect.

Motor tics are common in children; between 4% and 10% of children will have a transient tic that may last for several weeks or even a few months. These tics usually disappear spontaneously. The tic may make the child and her parents anxious and may be stressful, but it passes quickly and has no psychological significance or long-term effect on a child's mental health.

Diagnosis can be difficult. The only way to diagnose a simple transient tic is in retrospect; we must wait to see whether it goes away. There is no way to tell from simply observing a tic or from medical or psychological examination whether it will disappear by itself or whether it is the beginning of a more serious disorder.

Not all odd or repetitive movements are tics; there are many other causes of abnormal movements. Only your doctor can make this distinction.

Tics may develop as early as the preschool years, but 7 is the average age when tics are first diagnosed. At first, the child typically has a single tic, which is indistinguishable from benign tics that will disappear.

For some children the tic may change. For example, a child may start out with blinking eyes. After several weeks the tic may stop, but it may be followed by nodding or jerking the head. At times, two or more tics may occur together.

Vocal tics usually appear after motor tics. The most common vocal tics are throat clearing and coughing. At first, such tics may escape notice because they appear to result from a recent cold. Parents or teachers do not become concerned until they note that the coughing or throat clearing has gone on for many weeks, longer than could be explained by a cold.

In some children, the vocalizations change to grunting or barking noises. They may also appear as high-pitched cries, belching, or hiccuping. About one-fourth of children will have some form of vocal tic that includes vulgar or obscene words.

The following descriptions summarize how the *Diagnostic and Statistical Manual* of the American Psychiatric Association defines Tourette's syndrome, chronic motor or vocal tic disorder, and transient tic disorder.

Tourette's Syndrome

1. Both multiple motor and one or more vocal tics have been present at some time during the illness, although not necessarily concurrently.

2. The tics occur many times a day (usually in bouts), nearly every day, or intermittently throughout a period of more than 1 year.

3. The anatomic location, number, frequency, complexity, and severity of the tics change over time.

4. Onset occurs before age 21.

5. The disorder is not caused by drugs or by known central nervous system disease.

Chronic Motor or Vocal Tic Disorder

1. Either motor or vocal tics, but not both, have been present at some time during the illness.

2. The tics occur many times a day, nearly every day, or intermittently throughout a period of more than 1 year.

3. Onset occurs before age 21.

4. The disorder is not caused by drugs or by known central nervous system disease.

Transient Tic Disorder

1. Single or multiple motor and/or vocal tics are present.

2. The tics occur many times a day or nearly every day for at least 2 weeks, but for no longer than 12 consecutive months.

3. There is no history of Tourette's syndrome or chronic motor or vocal tic disorder.

4. Onset occurs before age 21.

5. The disorder is not caused by drugs or by known central nervous system disease.

In addition to the symptoms listed, other symptoms occur. These include increased irritability, distractibility, motor restlessness, and impulsivity. About one-third of children with Tourette's syndrome also have a learning disability. We must be alert to these symptoms because the same behaviors can bring ADHD to our attention.

Anywhere from 30% to 50% of children with Tourette's syndrome also have symptoms that meet the criteria for diagnosis of ADHD. Unfortunately, our knowledge is insufficient to help us understand the meaning of this overlap in symptoms. We do not know whether ADHD and Tourette's syndrome are discrete, separate disorders that only coincidentally have symptoms that appear to overlap, or whether we are mistaken when we diagnose a child with Tourette's syndrome as having ADHD because the child is impulsive or distractible or has a short attention span.

This dilemma takes on increased importance when we consider the relationship between treatment of ADHD with psychostimulants and Tourette's syndrome. In the early 1980s, research reports from several medical centers suggested that some children developed Tourette's syndrome when treated with psychostimulants, especially Ritalin. It appeared that Tourette's syndrome might be a side effect of treatment with Ritalin.

In most cases, the symptoms of Tourette's syndrome vanished when treatment with Ritalin was discontinued. In a few cases, however, the symptoms did not disappear, and Tourette's syndrome had to be treated with other medications.

Research and clinical experience during the past few years call into question the earlier conclusion that Tourette's syndrome is a side effect of treatment with psychostimulants. It is possible that patients who developed Tourette's syndrome were mistakenly diagnosed as having ADHD because of the overlapping symptoms. Remember that ADHD is often neglected and not diagnosed accurately. Tourette's syndrome occurs considerably less frequently than ADHD. If an error in diagnosis is made, it is more likely that someone will misdiagnose ADHD rather than Tourette's syndrome. Thus, if the more typical signs of Tourette's syndrome, as set out above, appear in a child who has been diagnosed as having ADHD and who has been treated with a psychostimulant, these signs may not be a side effect of the drug but simply the emergence of Tourette's syndrome at a later stage of symptoms.

Despite speculation and continuing research in this area, there is still no conclusive evidence one way or the other. Consequently it is important to remain vigilant in observing any patient under treatment with a stimulant to note the emergence of any symptoms that might suggest a tic disorder. If a child develops these symptoms, it is the practice of most physicians to immediately discontinue the use of the psychostimulant.

Parents often find it difficult to discontinue medicine when their child has benefited from it. Stopping the medication usually causes a recurrence of learning and behavioral problems. Children can be treated with other drugs, such as antidepressants or Clonidine, but neither drug is as effective as the psychostimulants in treating ADHD.

The implications for parents and educators are clear. Any child with ADHD who is being treated with a psychostimulant should be watched carefully. The appearance of motor or vocal tics should be immediately brought to the attention of the child's physician. Any suspicious tic-like behavior, including a cough or throat clearing that does not go away in the normal course of time, should be treated seriously and brought to the doctor's attention.

TREATING PRESCHOOLERS WITH MEDICINE

Although we are satisfied that children with ADHD can be treated safely and effectively with medication, most of us tend to be cautious in our use of medication, especially with preschool children. To make a decision about treating a 4-year-old with medication, we must first consider how the diagnosis is made for a child this age.

How old must a child be to make a reliable diagnosis of ADHD? Keep in mind that there are no medical or psychological tests for ADHD. We have a number of measures that give an indication of how well a child pays attention, how distractible he might be, and even to what extent the child can control impulses. None of these tests point directly at a diagnosis of ADHD. There are a number of reasons why a child might be inattentive, distractible, or impulsive. Tests provide useful information, but an informed clinician can arrive at a reliable diagnosis only by integrating test information with a careful and detailed description of the child's history and pattern of behavior.

Even the most experienced psychologist or pediatrician depends on clinical judgment to reach a diagnosis and a decision about consequent treatment. It stands to reason that children with more severe symptoms will be recognized earlier and diagnosed more easily. For example, one mother described her son's behavior in this way: "He never walked. One day he pulled himself up and started running, and he hasn't stopped." It is easy to diagnose children who are hyperactive from such an early age and who are active all the time.

Another preschool child, who may be just as inattentive but not hyperactive, is less likely to be seen as a problem early in life. Consequently, she is less likely to be brought to the attention of professionals. Even when she is examined by a physician, her parents are likely to be reassured because her behavior in the examining room is not remarkable. Usually the pediatrician tells the parents that they are fortunate to have a normal, healthy girl "with a lot of life in her."

The child's youth may serve as a barrier to early diagnosis. We must look for well-established patterns of behavior; these patterns emerge more clearly from the history of a child who has lived 8 years than from the history of a 3-year-old.

In chapter 1 we discussed some of the barriers to early recognition and diagnosis of ADHD. They include lack of awareness among many people about the significance of the symptoms of this disorder. Children with ADHD are often dismissed as "all boy" or as "immature." The question, "How early can we diagnose ADHD?" must be answered: "It depends on how severe the symptoms are."

Despite the difficulty we may have in recognizing ADHD, it is not unusual to make the diagnosis in children as young as 3 years of age. An extremely active child may be diagnosed earlier, but most child psychologists are cautious about labeling young children. Psychologists are more likely to try to help parents live with the troublesome behavior.

Once the diagnosis has been made, a plan of treatment must be developed; this plan may include counseling for the parents, guidance in child management, establishment of behavior modification programs, planning for preschool, socialization experiences, and, in some cases, use of medicine.

Medication can be helpful with preschool children, but side effects may be more severe in younger children. For reasons no one can explain, many children respond well to Ritalin, Dexedrine, or Cylert once they are 5 or 6 years old, but at 3 or 4, they either do not respond or they experience side effects that make the medication difficult to use.

The indications for using medication with preschoolers are the same as those for older children, adolescents, and adults. To what extent does the ADHD interfere with the child's normal life? With preschool children we need not be concerned about the effect the ADHD symptoms have on school learning. We should consider the use of medication if the symptoms of ADHD create serious family problems or if the child is unhappy to the extent that his mental health suffers.

Most children with ADHD who require medication must take it for a long time, so we put off using it if possible. We are not inordinately concerned about using medicine over a long period, but it is simple common sense to avoid using any drugs that are not absolutely essential. Therefore, we recommend that you make every effort to look for alternatives before beginning drug therapy.

If your child's behavior causes a health or safety risk, or if it creates so much tension in the family that you are all miserable most of the time, serious consideration must be given to the use of medication.

In our efforts to help parents decide about the use of medicine in treating their preschool child with ADHD, we have found that two major concerns lead them to consider medication. Most parents are extremely cautious about treating their children with medication at this age; often they do so only with reluctance, even when it is clearly necessary.

Parents frequently express concern for a child's safety because they find that they cannot keep her in the house, even with the front door locked. Once outside, they cannot be sure she will not run away or dart into the street.

Social situations are also a problem. Visiting friends and family is impossible. Family activities are often filled with so much conflict and stress that no one has a good time. Outings that start with high hopes end in tears and recriminations. These problems are of special concern to parents when their child is aggressive. Many parents find it difficult to deal with their child when he hits, kicks, or bites other children or even adults and animals.

The second concern that leads most often to the use of medication for preschool children is the realization that parents have fallen into a destructive way of trying to control their child. The child's entire life may seem to be negative because of frequent criticism by parents, siblings, neighbors, and relatives. Parents worry about the effect of this assault on the child's self-concept.

One mother described her 4^1/$_2$-year-old daughter by saying, "It seems we are always yelling at her and sending her to her room when she is at home. At preschool, her teachers always correct her. She knows the other children don't want to play with her and sometimes comes home from school crying because other children don't like her."

We will have more to say about self-concept in chapter 6, but parents are wise to pay particular heed to the child's developing self-image; it is easier to prevent damage than to heal wounds already made.

What should we expect from medical treatment of preschool children with ADHD? Some interesting research has been conducted by Russell Barkley at the University of Massachusetts Medical Center. He has written a number of important books and articles, many dealing with behavioral management of children with ADHD. Recently he reported on the effects of Ritalin on the way preschool children get along with their mothers.

Barkley studied 27 children with ADHD and their mothers. The study included 19 boys and 8 girls, ranging from about $2^1/_2$ to $4^1/_2$ years old. Barkley and his co-workers gave the children either Ritalin or identical placebo tablets and then videotaped the children in a wide variety of activities that included their mothers.

During free play, mothers of children who were taking Ritalin gave their children considerably fewer commands than those whose children were not taking medication. Barkley hypothesized that when the mothers observed that their children did not require as much control or direction, they did not have to issue as many commands.

The research workers also studied mothers and children in situations where the children had to engage in specific tasks. During these tasks, children on medication were more compliant, showing a 45% decrease in undesirable behaviors; the mothers made significant reductions in controlling and in negative responses to their children.

These mothers did not know whether their children were taking medication or the placebo at any particular point in the study. The study design made it clear that the mothers did not simply decide to be more cooperative or less critical because they were participating in this experiment. Mothers remained more critical of their children when the children were receiving the placebo instead of Ritalin.

We see the two benefits in the results. By actual measurement, the children on medicine were more compliant; they displayed less negative, disruptive, and off-task behavior. At the same time, the mothers' controlling and negative comments were reduced; this outcome, along with experience of success, should have a positive effect on the children's feelings about themselves.

As helpful as medicine can be for preschool children, our clinical experience and the results of several careful research studies make it clear that many children 2 to 5 years of age either do not benefit from medication or suffer side effects to an extent that makes the medication impossible to use. Over 70% of all children with ADHD over age 6 respond well to psychostimulants, but only about one-half of preschoolers do. We do not know why such a difference exists, but many children who do not benefit from medication in their early years obtain a great deal of help from medication when they are older.

3

Effective Communication Among Family, School, and Physician

Good communication is essential among those who care for the child with attention deficit–hyperactivity disorder, but there are many barriers to cooperation. One of the most significant obstacles arises from the fact that often no single person is designated as the primary coordinator for all forms of treatment. Consequently teachers, physician, parents, and other concerned individuals seem to work almost independently. Although they may communicate with each other and share information or written reports, they do not come together in a way that allows for cooperative planning.

The makeup of the team that takes care of the child depends on the child's needs. The team for the child who is taking medication must include his physician; if the child is receiving psychological treatment, the therapist must be included. Teachers and parents are always team members.

COMMUNICATION AMONG TEAM MEMBERS

At the outset we must understand what types of information the team members need from each other. We then will discuss the importance of information from school in the physician's diagnosis of ADHD. Finally, if a child needs medication, we will see how data from school are used to adjust the dosage.

Physicians generally have three sources of information available when they evaluate or treat a patient with any ailment: the findings from a physical examination, the results of any laboratory tests that were conducted, and the history—that is, background information and the patient's account of what is wrong. Now consider the information available to a physician who is examining a child for the first time and is faced with the possibility of ADHD. First, the physical examination usually offers the doctor very little useful information. In most cases there are no specific detectable signs or symptoms that help a physician to diagnose or rule out ADHD. Moreover, the child's behavior during the examination may not tell the doctor anything because many hyperactive children can sit quietly for a few minutes in the doctor's office. Similarly, many normal children may appear quite restless at times.

In a recent study, a large group of pediatricians was asked what factors helped them to diagnose and treat ADHD. Only 29% said that they used the physical examination at all. Even among those who did use findings from a physical examination as a source of information, most acknowledged that there usually was nothing useful in the examination. The physical examination has very limited value in diagnosing ADHD because the symptoms of the disorder are primarily behavioral, not physical. In fact, if we set the child's behavior aside for a moment, we see that there are absolutely no physical signs or symptoms that allow the doctor to diagnose ADHD or to rule it out conclusively.

Of course, if a child is very active in the doctor's office and this observation is combined with the parents' reports of hyperactivity, the doctor usually can make the diagnosis with ease. Most children, however, are not that easy to diagnose.

In addition, there are no laboratory tests to aid the doctor in diagnosing ADHD. No physical tests, psychological tests, or any other sorts of tests exist to make the diagnosis. Some tests are helpful in quantifying the degree of a child's inattentiveness or activity level, but those tests are merely descriptive. They allow us to rate the child on distractibility or activity but they do not allow us to determine the cause of the attention problem or high level of activity. An anxious child who cannot concentrate might score just as high on these tests or higher than a child who has ADHD. Therefore, the doctor has no tests that lead to a diagnosis of ADHD, in contrast to the variety of medical and physical tests that help in the diagnosis of other problems.

Thus, two-thirds of the information on which a doctor usually relies when examining a patient, physical examination and laboratory tests, are not available. As a result, the physician must rely exclusively on the history given by the patient and/or the patient's parents. Doctors are well aware of this situation. Although only 29% of doctors surveyed looked to the physical examination for help in diagnosis, 93% said that the history from parents was important and 89% said that the history from teachers was important. Eighty-three percent also said that they relied on psycho-educational reports from school psychologists or from special education consultants in the child's school.

Let us look further at the third main source of information, the history obtained from parents. In the case of a child who may be very impulsive or hyperactive, the parents' history certainly will point the doctor toward a diagnosis of ADHD. Some children are especially active even while they are still in the womb. Children who hit the ground running and never stop are easy to diagnose.

In other cases a child's behavior may not have been particularly disturbing to parents at home; the parents only come to the doctor's office because of school-related difficulties. In these cases the parents may be giving information that is not based on first-hand experiences with their own child but is a second-hand report of the teacher's observations in the classroom. This situation denies the doctor the opportunity to question the parents in greater detail, as would be possible if the parents were describing their own experiences.

In view of the circumstances under which most physicians are asked to make a diagnosis of ADHD, it should not be surprising that many children whose symptoms are not especially clear-cut either are never diagnosed or are diagnosed only after long bouts of repeated school learning or behavioral problems. In fact, it should be gratifying to most parents to find that so many children are diagnosed accurately under these circumstances; they can credit it to the commitment of time and attention that most doctors are willing to give their young patients.

This review of the information that a physician uses to reach a diagnosis to plan treatment provides some guidelines for the types of information that parents and educators should try to give the doctor at the initial examination when a diagnosis of ADHD is being considered.

WHAT THE DOCTOR WOULD LIKE TO KNOW FROM THE TEACHER

Teachers, school psychologists, social workers, and counselors will have to take the initiative in providing some of this information to the physician. This initiative is necessary not because of the physician's neglect-

or lack of interest in information from the school but because many physicians are not familiar with the routines and practices in the school. Although a doctor may ask for a report card or information that can be provided on a brief rating scale, most doctors do not know enough about how a classroom operates to ask for anything else. Until the teacher educates the doctor, the doctor usually remains unaware of the rich supply of information that can be provided by the school.

It is also important for teachers to give this information to the child's physician in a form that the physician can understand and use. It is rarely sufficient to instruct a parent to take a child to the family doctor to "see if he has an attention deficit–hyperactivity disorder or is hyperactive." In some cases such a referral may lead to an accurate diagnosis, but, as many educators are aware, often the visit to the doctor's office yields no diagnosis or no useful recommendations for treatment.

We recommend that instead of merely sending the parents and the child to the doctor, the teacher (and any other school professionals who have had contact with the child) should prepare a package of materials along the lines described below and send that in addition. This package will give the physician abundant information that will help him or her to determine whether the child has ADHD. If the materials provided by the school are comprehensive, well organized, and to the point, they will serve as a substitute for the laboratory tests and direct observations that are not available to the physician.

We suggest that the teacher write a letter that can be mailed in advance to the doctor or that the parent can take to the appointment. Of course, this letter must meet with the approval and permission of the child's parents. In the letter, the teacher should explain why he or she believes that the child might have ADHD.

Here is an example of such a letter.

Dear Doctor _____:

I have had several meetings with Mr. and Mrs. Smith about their son John's progress in my second-grade classroom. We have discussed the possibility that John might have an attention deficit–hyperactivity disorder (ADHD).

Enclosed is a copy of the diagnostic criteria for ADHD. I have noted the parents' responses in column 1 and the results of my observations in column 2. I am also including a copy of the Conners' Teacher Rating Scale, which I filled out today.

I think John is a capable student, but he seldom completes his work. His work tends to be rushed and sloppy. At other times, he completes things but does not hand in his papers.

On tests John demonstrates that he knows the material; however, he does not seem to be able to concentrate in class. It seems that he cannot listen to directions. He must have something in his hands or be in movement frequently, and he walks around the classroom a great deal. At times he crawls on the floor, and at other times he calls out, talks, or yells in class for no apparent reason. It seems that he has not learned to control his behavior, and he is quite impulsive. His classmates dislike him because of frequent fights and his efforts to tease them.

I note that the Smith family has a possible history of ADHD. Mr. Smith told me that he was diagnosed as hyperactive when he was in school and is still this way. Mr. Smith's brother and father were also described as active both as children and as adults. To my knowledge, they did not receive medical attention for these symptoms.

I thought it appropriate to send you this letter because of the family history and because John's behavior in my classroom suggests a possible diagnosis of ADHD. If you would like any further information, Mr. and Mrs. Smith have instructed me to provide you with anything you might need. You are welcome to contact me at my office.

Sincerely,

There are three essential elements in this letter and in the materials that the teacher is sending along with the letter. First, the definition of ADHD, annotated with observations by teacher and parent, is valuable. This is objective information; it speaks to the doctor in terms of the diagnostic criteria for the disorder. In providing this information, the teacher has not overstepped the boundaries and intruded into the doctor's medical domain but has summarized the symptoms in terms of a medical diagnosis that should be familiar to the doctor.

The Conners' rating scale describes the child's behavior in a way that the doctor is likely to recognize. The Conners' scale is a helpful instrument because it is used widely in clinical research. A month rarely passes when one of the leading pediatric, child psychiatry, or family practice medical journals does not contain an article about ADHD in which the Conners' scale is used.

The Conners' scale provides a quantitative index, a number, that can be used as a reference in the future if the child is treated with medication or with behavior modification programs. The index will help us see how far we have come and whether our treatment has been effective.

The third element in the letter is essentially a summary of the teacher's observations. The teacher can prepare a daily log and summarize it for the doctor or can send the log itself. This is a behavioral description of the child. It overlaps the definition and the Conners' scale, but it also provides an opportunity to demonstrate the richness and complexities of the child's behavior that might be lost if only the first two items are used.

The letter can be written by a teacher, a principal, a counselor, a social worker, or a school psychologist. It does not matter who writes it; what matters is that the material is prepared and is provided to the physician. Keep in mind the importance of submitting a behavioral description to the doctor in a format the doctor understands.

Many children who are referred to physicians with a question of ADHD have been tested already by a school psychologist or a learning disability consultant. They may have had other special tests as well. Doctors usually want to know the results of such tests, but we have found that most test reports usually are too technical, are bogged down in jargon, and are unnecessarily wordy. It is a rare physician who has the time to read a four- or five-page report. (Some reports are even longer.) These test results may be sent along as a supplement to the basic material that we recommend here, but they are never a substitute. The standard psychological report written after a psychological evaluation by a school psychologist is always of some interest to a child's physician, but by itself it rarely helps the doctor to make the diagnosis of ADHD.

The value of the letter, the rating scale, and the other material is not limited to the time when the diagnosis is made. If a child is diagnosed as having ADHD, the doctor now has a substantial body of information describing the child's behavior before treatment is begun. This information provides an interesting and important reference point to which future descriptions of the child's behavior may be compared in order to assess the effectiveness of treatment.

DETERMINING DOSAGE

Once the diagnosis is made and the doctor prescribes medication, there remains the problem of determining the proper dosage. Here again, the doctor needs detailed school information because it is impossible to calculate in advance the dosage for most drugs used to treat ADHD. There is no way for the doctor to know what dose of medicine will be most helpful. The physician and the parent want enough medicine to get the job done, but certainly no more than the child actually needs.

Therefore, in most cases, the child's doctor will begin treating ADHD with as small a dose as possible, possibly 5 mg of Ritalin in the morning and at lunchtime. After observing the child's behavior for several weeks on that dose, the doctor will gradually increase the medication to higher levels until the desired therapeutic effect is obtained or until it becomes clear to the doctor that further increases will not help. The more information the doctor has at each stage of this process, the more precise the decisions about the dosage can be.

Fortunately, most children respond to relatively modest doses of psychostimulants, and it is fairly easy to gain control of their learning and behavioral difficulties. Yet even for those children, several adjustments of dosage may be necessary over a period of 2 to 6 weeks. For substantial numbers of children, however, the process of regulating the dosage and even of selecting the most effective medication can take a number of months. Any process that requires such a long time will also require good understanding, patience, and persistence on the part of everyone who is participating. It has been our experience that three members of the team usually are involved at this point: The parent, teacher, and physician work together far more effectively and with much better results if communication among them is open and generous. If the physician is not receiving detailed information about a child, he or she may be reluctant to continue to prescribe and change drugs and to adjust the dosage over many months.

There is another reason to make every effort to collect detailed information on a child's behavior and to make sure that everyone involved in working with the child has access to it. Over the past few years we have learned that some children require different doses of medication for control of the different symptoms of ADHD. The amount of medicine necessary to control a child's hyperactivity, for example, may not be the same amount necessary to control impulsivity or short attention span. For many children, fortunately, the dose that works for one symptom also works for another, but we never know that in advance.

Consequently, some children who finally come to do quite well behaviorally still do not achieve well in school. We will discuss the relationship between use of medication and academic achievement in chapter 5. Here we want to remind you that a child's behavior may be brought under control after several months of careful adjustment in dosage, but if we wait several more months and find that the child's achievement is not keeping pace with the improvement in behavior, we face the additional task of further changes in dosage in order to gain as much benefit as possible both in behavior and in learning. Once again we want to emphasize that this goal can be accomplished only with a great deal of cooperation.

Parents and teachers are often unsure how far they should go in providing information for the physician. In some cases teachers are not certain how well their ideas will be received by the child's doctor; often teachers as well as parents are reluctant to intrude into what they regard as the doctor's territory.

Most physicians who work with children welcome any additional information that teachers can provide. Occasionally a physician will be impatient with the teacher's effort to provide information, claiming that the teacher is intruding into medical matters that are of no concern to anyone other than the physician, but such an uncooperative, uninformed attitude is quite rare.

Even so, many doctors will not take the initiative to ask for more than a brief report of what the child is doing. In the latest edition of one standard pediatrics textbook, pediatricians are urged to obtain reports from the school every 5 to 7 days during the time when they are trying to regulate the dosage of the medication to treat ADHD. It is a rare physician who follows this guideline, but many doctors send a questionnaire to the school before beginning medical treatment and ask for follow-up reports on the same questionnaire.

The questionnaire that doctors use most often is the Conners' rating scale, but others are useful as well. Physicians also may ask a child's parents about general behavior and academic performance, but beyond requesting that an occasional questionnaire be filled out, most doctors simply do not know what to ask the teacher to report. Therefore, someone in the school—the classroom teacher, the counselor, or the consultant— must take the initiative to pull together the kinds of information we have discussed in this chapter and send to them to the doctor.

Who should take the responsibility for coordinating this communication system? Often it is a simple matter of a telephone call or a brief letter, but in other cases the task can be quite complex and time-consuming. A great number of telephone calls and frequent, consistent efforts may be needed to share information from the home and the classroom with everyone else on the treatment team. No single individual necessarily does the job best; it can be accomplished by the classroom teacher, the special education teacher, the consultant, the social worker, the counselor, the school nurse, or a parent. The problem is usually that no one is assigned to the job of coordinator, so someone has to take the responsibility on his or her own initiative.

Two main problems arise. First, because there are no clear-cut lines of authority and responsibility, many of the people involved simply assume that someone else will be coordinating the child's care. In many cases it does not even occur to anyone that the job is available and that someone should fill it.

There is another major barrier to coordination: Most people do not believe that the other members of the informal team would welcome or even accept their assumption of the coordinator's role. We have spoken to many teachers, for example, who fear that physicians, psychologists, and others might not welcome them in that position. One teacher asked, "How can I tell a doctor that he or she ought to pay more attention to my reports of a child's behavior in the classroom?"

Of course we all feel sensitive about intruding into the domain of another professional. Many people are equally concerned when they think that someone with less experience or knowledge than theirs is trying to tell them what to do. These concerns, however, need not be a barrier to a school professional or parent who seizes the initiative and says, "I will coordinate these activities."

In our own practice we heartily welcome any information we receive from a child's school. We know that we speak for the majority of pediatricians, family practitioners, and other psychologists in encouraging someone to take the responsibility for this type of coordination.

Behavioral Management

This chapter on behavioral management begins with a discussion of a number of principles that explain how behavior is learned and how it can be changed. These principles are called *behavioral* because the emphasis is on observable behavior with no special concern about the underlying feelings and attitudes. It would be wrong, of course, to think that we can ignore a person's feelings and pay attention only to behavior, but, at times, it is useful to make this distinction because it makes our task of managing children easier and more straightforward.

We will describe a step-by-step program for behavioral change that includes methods for increasing desirable behavior and decreasing undesirable behavior; there are some behaviors we want our children to start or continue and others we want them to stop.

BEHAVIORAL PRINCIPLES

After reading several paragraphs of this section, you may be tempted to skip ahead, because what you are reading will seem no more than common sense. We urge you to continue reading. Much of what we will discuss here will be somewhat familiar; nonetheless, we have found that

57

principles of learning and habit formation must be understood in considerable detail if we are to apply them effectively. The reasons for this will become clear when we move to the section in chapter 5 on how children with ADHD learn. Subtle or small errors in the way we set up a behavioral management program for a youngster with ADHD often account for the failure of that program. There is a thin line between success and failure, and we want to do everything possible to increase the chances for success.

There are only a few principles of learning with which we need to be concerned. First, several definitions are necessary. Let us start with the term *behavior.* We all know what the word means, but we need a precise definition. Too often parents think they are describing behavior when they are not. For example, we often ask parents what behaviors of their child with ADHD irritate them the most. We commonly hear, "He is so angry and mean with his little sister." On further questioning, it becomes clear that the parents know the exact behaviors they are referring to, but "anger" is not a behavior. Anger is a feeling, and saying that a child is "mean to his sister" is an interpretation of what the child is doing. We usually follow these statements with a question such as "Tell me what specific behavior causes you to say that he is angry or being mean." This usually results in a description of the behavior, not an attitude or feeling. For example, the child may have hit his younger sister. He may have made angry faces or said nasty things. These are examples of behavior. They can be seen or heard.

Words used to describe a child may sound behavioral but may actually be offering an interpretation or opinion. For example, we frequently encounter parents or teachers who say that a child is hyperactive or, simply, overactive. These are descriptions of behavior. It is usually necessary, however, to go a step farther and ask what exact behaviors caused them to say that their child is hyperactive. Different types of behavior in different people result in different definitions of hyperactivity. For instance, an impatient, intolerant, or passive teacher might interpret normal exuberance and enthusiasm in a kindergarten child as hyperactivity. This is why it is important that we describe the behavior itself. That is the starting place. We must all talk about the same thing to communicate clearly and to set up the best behavioral management program.

Two other technical words require definition—*reinforcement* and *extinction.* A *reinforcement* or *reinforcer* is normally a reward. The terms refer to anything that increases the probability that a certain behavior will become more frequent. We can reinforce a child's cooperative behavior with a younger sibling by giving her a tangible reward, such as a toy or a piece of candy, or an intangible reward, such as love or praise. The latter reinforcer is often more potent. Saying to your child, "That makes me proud" or "I'm very pleased to see what you did with your brother" are intangible reinforcers.

Much reinforcement is provided by parents, teachers, or other children. Some reinforcement, however, is intrinsic. This means that it comes from within the person, or that the act we desire is rewarding in itself. Many types of success are intrinsically rewarding. The jogger who increases his distance from 1 to 2 miles may feel very proud of himself and be motivated to get out the next day and do it again. He does not need someone else to tell him how well he has done.

Similarly, the child who takes a cookie when her mother is not watching has that behavior reinforced by eating a tasty treat. Punching a younger brother or sister and causing a cry of pain may please a jealous child with ADHD who feels rejected and treated worse than the younger child. The reward from the pleasure of revenge may be very powerful and cause the punching behavior to continue, even in the face of strong disapproval or punishment. In other words, the child's reward from the behavior is more powerful than the punishment used by the parents to eliminate the behavior. This is why it is so important to understand the nature of the reinforcement. It helps us to understand why it can be illogical or nonsensical. One of the first steps to changing behavior is to understand why it is reinforcing for a child.

Lying is a good example. Why does your child persist in lying about incomplete schoolwork when he knows that you are going to find out the truth sooner or later? Your child knows that he will have twice the trouble, because it is not just the incomplete schoolwork that upsets you, but also the lies that were told.

Examine these events from the child's point of view to see what reinforces lying. Your child probably fears your response if he confesses to unfinished assignments. You may insist that he stay in the house until the work is done and you probably will get angry. Your anger makes your son upset and nervous. By lying, he avoids your displeasure; avoiding your anger makes him less anxious, and escape from anxiety is a very good feeling. Reduction of anxiety will reinforce just about any behavior. This is why your child lies. Judgment day is off in the future. Anxiety is low. The lie reduces anxiety, so the habit becomes stronger. It may not initially make sense to you, but viewed from a behavioral perspective with an understanding of reinforcement principles, the lies are a logical response to the circumstances.

No behavior will continue if it is not reinforced. The reason bad habits or annoying behaviors persist is because they are reinforced in some way we do not fully understand. If we eliminate all reinforcement, the behavior will cease. This process is referred to as *extinction*. We can extinguish undesirable behavior by never rewarding or reinforcing it. This is an easy principle to state, but figuring out all the things that reinforce behavior and then finding ways to ensure that the behavior will not be reinforced is far more complex and difficult.

In discussing the preceding definitions, we have introduced several principles of learning that are the foundation of what we know about learning behavior and habit formation. These principles can be stated concisely. Behavior must be reinforced or it will not be learned. If you eliminate all reinforcement, learned behavior will be extinguished.

Several other principles should be noted. Behavior that is learned on a partial reinforcement schedule is more resistant to extinction than behavior that is learned with 100% reinforcement. An illustration should make this clear. Consider a 4-year-old child put to bed at 8:30 P.M. The child's bedroom is down the hall from the living room, where both parents are reading or watching television. The child knows that he risks a reprimand from his parents and possibly a smack on the rear end if he comes into the living room, but he does not want to stay in bed.

To find a way to delay sleep and get his parents' attention, he calls for a drink of water. As soon as he asks for a drink, his mother goes into the kitchen, gets a glass of water, and brings it to him; the child drinks it, and having accomplished his purpose, he settles down and eventually goes to sleep. He has learned a powerful lesson. The following night he does the same thing and his mother responds in the same way. As soon as the child calls, his mother brings a glass of water. In a short time, the ritual of asking for and receiving a glass of water is firmly established and the child does it every night. His mother is mildly irritated, but she can live with it.

Consider another hypothetical family. The same circumstances apply. This family also includes a 4-year-old child who doesn't like her 8:30 bedtime. This child's parents have a different approach to managing bedtime delays, however. When the child calls for water, both father and mother ignore her. They know that if they ignore her long enough, eventually she will stop nagging.

Unfortunately, repeated requests for water are irritating and disruptive. Sometimes the parents can ignore the calls, but at other times it is easier, after the child has asked for water a half-dozen times, to give in. She, like her age-mate described before, also learns an effective technique for delaying bedtime; the ritual of getting a glass of water becomes established in her life as well.

The first child asked for a glass of water and the reinforcement (attention and water) occurred every time. This habit was learned at a 100% rate of reinforcement. The second child might have called for a glass of water 10 times before her mother appeared at her bedside. This child had to work

10 times as hard. She learned that she will not get water every time she asks. She may not know that she has been reinforced 10% of the time, but she does know that sometimes she will ask for water and not get anything. The second child has learned her habit with a partial reinforcement schedule.

Most human behavior is learned through partial reinforcement. This behavior is much harder to extinguish than behavior learned with 100% reinforcement. The reason is simple.

Imagine that both sets of parents now decide that things have gone far enough; they are fed up with the bedtime-drink ritual, and they are going to break the habit. The parents of the first child staunchly resolve to tell him that there will be no more drinks after he gets into bed. They commit themselves to make no response to requests for water.

If the family is typical, the child responds to the new rule by ignoring it. The request for water may be delayed the first night, but eventually it comes. The parents hang on and ignore him, and after a few more requests he settles down and falls asleep. The parents know the battle has not been won, but they are on the right track. The next night, the child tries again. The parents resist, and by the fourth or fifth night the child falls asleep quietly. He may ask for water again a week later, but if his parents are consistent, eventually the behavior is extinguished. All reinforcement has been removed.

The parents of our second child try the same thing. But they have a problem the first family did not have. Their child has learned persistence. The first child was used to getting reinforced every time. As soon as he was no longer getting water, he realized that things had changed. It was worth it to keep trying; after all, it did not take much energy to ask again for a glass of water, but it soon became clear that it would not work and so he stopped.

The second child, however, is used to working hard. She has had to call for water 10, 15, or even 20 times. Some nights she gets no response. She knows, though, that if she keeps at it, eventually she is going to get what she wants.

It is not uncommon for a child who has learned the habit on a partial reinforcement schedule to ask for water up to 50 times that first night. Perhaps her parents are wise enough, and in sufficient control of their own frustration, not to respond. Unfortunately, after a child calls out 50 times in an hour or two, most parents lose faith in their plan of ignoring the behavior; they go in to talk. They may give their child water to shut her up because "anything is better than having the whole evening ruined," or they may go into her bedroom and tell her that they are not going to give her water. They may even give her a spanking or a reprimand.

Either choice is unfortunate. In both cases the child has successfully captured her parents' attention. She is calling the tune. If the parents spank or severely reprimand her, they antagonize and arouse her further and interfere with the relaxation that should precede sleep. Heated feelings develop, frustration builds, and the parents feel guilty and angry. If this second family wants to extinguish the bedtime-drink ritual, they are going to have to work a lot longer than the first family because their child has learned to persevere.

Be careful. An attempt to eliminate behavior can actually lower the reinforcement schedule to a level that makes behavior harder than ever to extinguish. This occurs when parents firmly resolve not to give in, but eventually do. In this case, a child learns even greater perseverance. Whereas she might have been used to getting rewarded one-tenth of the time, she now learns that rewards only come every hundred times. If she persists, she will eventually get her way.

There is a very simple principle that emerges from all of this: Do not start an extinction program unless you are prepared to see it through.

DISTINCTION BETWEEN PUNISHMENT AND EXTINCTION

Punishment suppresses undesirable behavior but under most conditions does not eliminate it. Extinction is a more systematic means of eliminating undesirable behavior. Also, punishment is usually connected in the child's mind with the punisher, so a child may stop undesirable behavior only when the person who gives the spanking is around.

Punishment also causes fear. When a child is punished he may stop doing what you want him to stop, which is fine, but he may also fear you, which you do not want. A child may learn to fear school or particular subjects when punishment is connected with them. There is no such thing as healthy fear. It may be sensible to teach your young child to fear fire or heavy traffic, but try to avoid causing fear whenever possible.

There are other disadvantages to the use of punishment. Punishment involves an aggressive act toward the child. Children view their parents and teachers as models. They copy their behavior. Children who are punished with force show more aggression with friends as well as toward their parents. An occasional single slap on the rear end may be a part of normal child rearing, but physical punishment that goes beyond that is ineffective and often creates additional problems.

An illustration is provided by the parent who spanks her child because the child has hit her sister. What do you suppose a child learns from a parent who tells her, "Hitting a person is no way to solve a problem," while at the same time hitting her? It is confusing and hypocritical, and it breeds angry resentment. Aggression that is either accepted or physically punished will increase. It must be extinguished in a systematic manner.

The frustration of raising a child with ADHD makes parents vulnerable to the use of physical punishment. Most parents admit that they physically punish their children, not so much because it is good for the child, but because the parents become angry and frustrated. Such acts may reduce parents' frustration but do not help the child. In fact, they usually are harmful. If you cannot handle the frustration your child creates with the procedures discussed in this book, talk to your family doctor. Perhaps psychological counseling will help you live more harmoniously with your child.

We recommend positive reinforcement and extinction as methods to change behavior. Reserve punishment for rare occasions. There are times when the consequences of a child's behavior are so dangerous that we risk hurting or frightening him. Take, for example, the impulsive child who dashes into a busy street. This behavior is best dealt with firmly and may require a spanking. Positive reinforcement for self-control and staying out of the street is an important part of management, but the first consideration must be the child's physical safety. Similarly, the 18-month-old child who insists on sticking metal objects into electric outlets has to be stopped even if this requires punishment.

Care must be taken not to injure a child. Spankings are exclamation points that might hurt a bit but that primarily serve to emphasize parents' displeasure. There are absolutely no circumstances when physical punishment should be used for revenge or to cause so much pain that the child seeks to avoid the pain in the future rather than the parents' disapproval.

Desirable behavior should be reinforced immediately, especially during the initial stages of any behavioral change process. When the newly acquired behavior reaches a satisfactory level, it should be reinforced intermittently. This will make the behavior more resistant to extinction. Tangible reinforcers are a good starting place, but they should quickly be replaced with social reinforcers.

Parents are often reluctant to give things to their children to reward desirable behavior. We have heard parents refer to this practice as "bribing" children, but if you think for a moment, you will see that the term "bribe" is not accurate. A bribe is something you give a person for doing something wrong or dishonest. For example, you may try to bribe your way out of trouble when you have committed a crime.

Giving a child a reward for doing something right is an excellent idea. When you get a reward for proper behavior, you are more likely to do it again. Despite the intrinsic reward of enjoying work, how many of us would return to our jobs day after day if we did not receive the tangible reinforcer of our wages or salary?

We recognize that you cannot continually reward a child for desirable behavior, so after the behavior becomes well established, you should substitute praise and encouragement for tangible reinforcers. We will discuss these procedures step by step later in this chapter.

DIFFERENCES IN THE LEARNING PRINCIPLES OF CHILDREN WITH ADHD

The principles of learning and habit formation we have been discussing apply to all children. Nonetheless, there are differences between the learning principles of children with ADHD and those of other children. In this section we will discuss some of these differences before moving on to consider their practical application.

Reinforcement Schedules

Normal children and those with ADHD learn equally well with 100% reinforcement. However, children with ADHD are less efficient learners on partial reinforcement schedules. The rule about persistence of habits learned on partial reinforcement also applies to children with ADHD. When we consider how children learn in the first place, we find that children with ADHD have a marked disadvantage: It takes them longer to learn in most instances. This delay in learning has nothing to do with the child's intelligence. Careful thought helps to clarify why the child with ADHD might learn more slowly.

In the early stages of learning, the rules children must follow and the habits they must establish are not clear, but if every time a child makes a correct response, the teacher says, "That's very good," the child knows what she is supposed to do. In this way, 100% reinforcement helps a child to organize events and to focus her attention.

On the other hand, a child with ADHD trying to learn a simple task in the classroom, from a teacher who is able to give only infrequent reinforcement, faces a partial schedule of reinforcement. Unfortunately, the child with ADHD does not always pay attention, even when the teacher gives occasional reinforcement or direction, and therefore the child suffers a learning handicap.

Timing of Reinforcement

Children with ADHD learn as well as other children when reinforcement is provided immediately. However, if there is a slight delay between the time the child acts and the time feedback or reinforcement are given, the child with ADHD learns much less efficiently than his peer without ADHD. The longer the interval between the behavior and reinforcement, the less efficiently the child with ADHD will learn. The reasons for this are complex and subtle, but one cause is easy to understand. The longer the interval between the action and the feedback, the more opportunity there is for a child's mind to skip to some other subject. By the time the reinforcement comes, whether it is in the form of a tangible reward, praise from the teacher, or even feedback information saying, "That's good. You did it right," the child's thoughts may be elsewhere.

Day-to-day habits, school learning, and other behavior actually consist of uncountable small segments. For example, the average first-grade child uses each new word four to five thousand times in speech and reading exercises before it becomes firmly implanted in her mind. Because these many fragments make up the complete learning experience, it is easy to see that the child with ADHD will be at a disadvantage compared to her classmates.

Contingent Versus Noncontingent Reinforcement

Contingent reinforcement makes clear to the child what the reinforcement is for. At the end of the day, a first-grade teacher may say, "You are behaving nicely, Billy." Alternatively, when he has his boots and coat on and is ready to go home, she may stop him at the door and say, "Billy, I'm very pleased with the way you dressed quickly, lined up, and waited for the other children to get ready." In the latter case, her praise is clearly contingent on the behavior. The connection should be drawn for the child. The child with ADHD learns more efficiently if the contingency is made explicit.

Who Paces the Task?

Many tasks we expect of children are governed by our own schedules. Others children can schedule for themselves. Do children with ADHD learn and perform more efficiently when they schedule their own work or when we schedule it for them? There are two answers to this question, because it depends on the task.

When a parent or teacher helps the child to pay attention and organize activities, the child does better when someone else paces the work. For example, if children are taking a spelling test and the teacher says, "All right now, class, the next word goes on line 2 and should be started at the left-hand margin, and the spelling word is . . . ," the child with ADHD will do as well as the others because the teacher's pacing helps keep him organized. If, however, the teacher's pacing of the task merely forces the children to do things on her schedule, the child with ADHD would be better off pacing the task himself.

Organization

Children with ADHD are more erratic in solving problems. This can be illustrated with an example. Imagine a checkerboard with 64 squares. Two people play a game. The squares are numbered and person A has to guess which square person B is thinking of. There is no trick to this game. Person A knows there are 64 squares. With the worst possible luck, A should not make more than 63 errors before guessing the correct square. The best way to ensure that you will have no more than 63 errors is to approach the task systematically. Each square can be guessed in an organized way. Start with the rows or with the columns, but work systematically. If you do not do this, with 64 squares, you might forget whether you have guessed a particular square, come back to it, and waste a turn.

Now think of your child with ADHD. If she is older than 9 or 10, this task might be easy for her, so she too would make no more than 63 errors. On the other hand, because of their difficulty in paying attention and their impulsivity, many children with ADHD cannot organize a logical, systematic method of attack for even as simple a task as this. On the average, children with ADHD make more errors at this guessing game than children who do not have ADHD.

If a child finds it difficult to organize this task, imagine what it must be like when he hears his teacher say, "Put away your reading book, take out your arithmetic book and a clean sheet of paper and a pencil, turn to page 38, number your sheet of paper from 1 to 10 down the left-hand margin, and do every other problem on the page. Work carefully and neatly and do the even problems if you get done early."

Have you ever sent your youngster on an errand with instructions such as, "Go up to your room, get your plaid shirt, stop in my bedroom at the sewing basket and get me a needle and thread and a yellow thimble, meet me in the living room, and I'll sew on that button for you"?

You know the frustration you experience when, after waiting in the living room for 10 minutes, you go to your son's bedroom and find him sitting on his bed looking through a book or listening to the radio. He got as far as his room and then became distracted. In fact, he probably does not remember what you asked him to do. "Oh yeah, I forgot," he says when you ask what he's doing.

It is easy to misinterpret this behavior as irresponsibility or even outright defiance. Your child probably was not paying careful attention in the first place and did not hear all the directions. His approach to the task is not much different from the random guessing in the checkerboard game. Since he had no clear goal in mind when he got to his room, he was easily distracted. He was probably honestly surprised when you marched into his room and asked what he had been doing while you were waiting for him downstairs.

These observations on how youngsters with ADHD learn not only suggest guidelines for how to help them organize themselves, but also what limitations we have to place on our expectations. Parents are often frustrated by these explanations of how children learn. Unless you know that there is a physical basis for these problems, it is easy to dismiss them as bad habits or laziness. After we explain to parents what we have been discussing here, many will nod their heads in acknowledgment, but they will then dismiss the explanations by commenting, "Well, that may all be true, but what it really comes down to is that she just wants things her own way."

It is sad when this happens because then it is easy to view your child as an adversary and to look at your relationship with her as a battle with a winner and a loser. That frame of reference in any family becomes a self-fulfilling prophecy. The normal habits of getting along and living with each other are turned into battles and the family home becomes a battleground. There usually is no winner at this level of conflict.

THE PROCESS OF BEHAVIORAL CHANGE

Specific steps are necessary to change behavior. What we will discuss here may seem obvious, but do not treat these matters lightly just because they seem like common sense. The more attention you give to following these instructions, the more likely you are to succeed.

The first step is to select the behavior you want to change. Remember our definition of behavior. To change behavior, you must be able to describe it clearly enough for another person to know what you are talking about. It is not helpful to say that you want to change your child's "attitude" or want to "make him more considerate" or "more responsible in the way he does schoolwork or chores around the house." It would be hard for a friend or neighbor to look at your child and tell what you meant by *attitude, consideration,* or *responsibility.* Instead, determine the specific behaviors your child engages in that cause you to label him inconsiderate, irresponsible, or a child with a bad attitude. These are the behaviors we want to change.

We recommend that you work on one segment of behavior or a small group of behaviors at a time. Do not be impatient or unrealistic in your expectations. More happens in these early stages than you may realize.

You will demonstrate to your child that you have both the means to control his behavior and the commitment to do it. You are going to improve your credibility and effectiveness. You are going to convince yourself that you are a good parent. All this can be accomplished by success in controlling only one or a small group of behaviors. The rest will come in time and will be accomplished more easily once the proper groundwork has been laid.

The behavior you choose to modify need not be the most troublesome or the most dramatic behavior you want to change. Select the behavior that you think you can successfully alter. It is best to do the easy work at the beginning. Success breeds success.

Choose an example. It might be a temper tantrum. It might be disruption at the dinner table. It could be interrupting when others are talking. Perhaps your 5-year-old chooses to make her most intrusive demands when you are on the telephone, in the bathroom, or busy at the kitchen stove. You might want to discourage your 8-year-old from pulling his 4-year-old sister's hair every time you are out of the room. Or, as one mother told us, "I think I'd be very happy with my life if he would just stop walking on the furniture and use the floor like everybody else."

Each example is easy to describe, and anyone looking at your child would be able to see the troublesome behaviors. Furthermore, these behaviors are easy to count. You can count the number of times your child interrupts when you are on the telephone. You can add up the number of times your son pulls his sister's hair. If you do not keep formal records of these behaviors, you still have a good idea of how often they occur. You will be able to evaluate the effectiveness of the behavioral change process.

There are several other considerations in selecting the target behavior for your first project. Choose behavior that occurs frequently. Disruptive behavior that occurs only three or four times a year, even if it is very serious or dangerous behavior, should not be your primary concern at this point. Also, choose behavior over which you have some control. For example, you have control over a young girl's temper tantrum because you can pick her up, carry her to her room, leave her there, and close and lock the door.

It is much more difficult to control behavior when the child is primarily responsible for it. For example, it is more difficult to influence your child to get dressed faster than it is for you to impose your will when he is having a temper tantrum. It is very difficult to "pull out" behavior from children. You know how obstructive children can be and how frustrating it is when you want them to hurry. To start, choose behavior over which you have control.

Methods for Increasing Desirable Behavior

In this section, we will consider the application of the principles that have already been learned. The most important thing is to apply rewards or reinforcement for behavior we want to improve. We know we must clearly identify the behavior and then select an appropriate reinforcer. The reinforcer has to be presented, initially, as closely as possible to 100% of the time. It must be contingent—that is, closely connected—to the behavior. Finally, we have to switch from 100% reinforcement to partial reinforcement.

Step 1. Select the behavior you want to change.   For purposes of illustration, imagine that you want to teach your 7-year-old child to sit quietly and not interrupt while the family is watching a half-hour television program.

Step 2. Select an appropriate reinforcer.   There are an unlimited number of choices to select that might be rewarding to a child. Some children can be rewarded with small amounts of food, such as candy or other treats. Colored stickers pasted on a sheet of paper are also rewards. Some children may be rewarded with 15 minutes of free time in which they can do as they like. This choice is particularly effective as a reward in the classroom. A very effective reward for young children is 15 minutes of undivided attention from their mother or father in which they can do anything they like.

Step 3. Set up the rules.   Explain carefully what you want done. Tell your daughter that you expect her not to interrupt from the time the television program starts until the first commercial. When the program resumes, she has to keep quiet again until the next commercial. Then she has to keep quiet until the end of the program. She can leave the room, but she cannot interrupt. The same sort of rules can be set for any behavior. They can be applied to taking out the garbage, completing schoolwork assignments, or any other behavior you want to increase in frequency and establish as a good habit.

Step 4. Explain to your child the connection between the rules and the reinforcer.   Point out that you have been to the store and purchased a package of stickers of small, brightly colored animals. Take a sheet of colored construction paper and mark it into small squares. Make clear to your child that every time she is successful and does not interrupt your television viewing, you and she together will get a sticker from the package and put it on the sheet of paper. Notice how this procedure meets our requirement for a 100% reinforcement schedule and also for contingent reinforcement. You are making it very clear exactly why you are doing what you are doing.

Step 5. Explain what happens next.   For many young children, selecting and pasting the stickers is sufficient reward in itself. You might, however, allow your child to qualify for a slightly larger prize when she has collected 10, 15, or 20 stickers. Tell her that when 20 stickers have been pasted on the page, you will take her to the store and buy her a small present for a dollar or less. Keep in mind that your child may not be successful every time. She may still interrupt.

In the early stages, it is important for you to make every effort to help your child be successful. If, for example, you notice that your child is going to interrupt and ruin her chance for a sticker, put your arm around her and put your finger across your pursed lips to remind her to keep quiet. Eventually we want her to do this on her own, but at first, we have to make sure that she achieves success. If she makes an error, interrupts, and does not earn a sticker for one particular segment, do not fuss about it. It is not necessary to remind her that she did not get her sticker. Instead, the next time she is successful, give her a sticker and praise her. Continually remind her how well she is doing and how pleased you are with her progress. Minimize her failures.

Step 6. Modifying the procedures.   It should eventually be possible to reduce the need for tangible reinforcers, such as the stickers, and substitute two intangible rewards: your praise and the child's sense of satisfaction for a job well done. This might take a long time. Many parents find that, after they have achieved some success with the stickers, they become a bit sloppy and neglect to follow through as carefully as they should. This is often associated with a resumption of the troublesome behavior. It is important for you to step back and take a look at your behavior modification program. Have you begun to get sloppy or have you changed the procedure? Too often parents and teachers misinterpret why the behavior recurs and think that the procedures "worked for a while, but then they didn't work any more." The procedures always work. The procedures will continue to be effective as long as they are implemented carefully.

When you are satisfied with your child's behavior (this might not be perfect behavior, but only behavior within tolerable limits), look for a way to fade out tangible reinforcers. Buy larger stickers. Substitute these stickers for the smaller ones, but give the larger sticker after a half-hour. In this way you are giving the reinforcer less frequently. Because you are giving a slightly larger reward, the child does not feel cheated. You are also switching to partial reinforcement to ensure behavior that will be more resistant to extinction.

If you follow these procedures, you will find that after another week or so, you can give your child a sticker every other day, an even lower percentage of reinforcement. After another week, nontangible rewards such as praise should be sufficient to maintain the behavior. If the objectionable behavior increases or there is a decrease in the positive behavior, do not hesitate to go back to an earlier step of the behavioral change process and institute a more consistent, more tangible reward at the necessary stage.

You might ask whether these elaborate procedures are worthwhile. They require more than casual commitment and effort. Is the payoff worth the effort? We think it is. First, you will find that if you help your child control his behavior in one set of circumstances, there will be a positive effect in other areas as well. You get a larger payoff than you might at first think.

Also, you prove to yourself that your child's behavior is under your control. You reduce some of the frustration and chaos in your own life. You do not feel as helpless, which creates a better mood for the entire family. It might even help you to better tolerate other disruptive behavior. Perhaps most important of all, behavior management gives your child an opportunity to control his own behavior to some extent. This should not only be a source of pride and satisfaction to him, but it should also reduce some of his anxiety as he begins to see that his behavior is not as bad or out of control as he might have feared.

Methods of Decreasing (Extinguishing) Undesirable Behavior

Increasing desirable behavior and decreasing undesirable behavior usually go together. However, at times, undesirable behavior is so disruptive that we do not have the luxury of trying to build up more positive behavior; we must first eliminate the objectionable behavior. For example, if a child is very disruptive at the dinner table or has such severe temper tantrums that they create a great deal of tension for everyone else, these behaviors should be the focus for extinction procedures.

Consider the need to eliminate a 5-year-old child's violent temper tantrums. Children learn tantrums the same way they learn other behaviors: because they get reinforced. Our first task is to identify what is rewarding the child who has a temper tantrum. Reinforcers vary from child to child and family to family, but many are similar.

Two general reinforcers keep temper tantrums going. First, the child gets what he wants. Temper tantrums can be terrifying. Even the most experienced and capable parents, in the face of tantrum rages that go on for hours, begin to lose confidence in their judgment and common sense. Perhaps the child is ill, they think. Maybe he is having a seizure or some sort of fit. What if you let him cry and go on like this for hours, and he develops trouble breathing or chokes? Parents fear that their child's "mind might snap." Children can and do hold their breath until they turn blue and pass out. Temper tantrums like this cannot be taken lightly.

Most parents have heard the commonsense wisdom that temper tantrums should be ignored. This is fine advice to give, but it is difficult to practice when your child is lying on the floor banging her head against the side of a table. Given the bewildering or violent behavior children incorporate into temper tantrums, it is not surprising that tantrums are an effective way to force parents to give children what they want.

The second major reinforcer for tantrum behavior is attention. A child can quite literally capture the full attention of every other human being within listening range with a loud, violent tantrum. If a child fails to get the toy or privilege he initially wanted, he can still successfully immobilize the household and direct all the family's attention to himself. The tantrum, in effect, says, "You may not give me what I want, but I can make your life so miserable that you'll think carefully about it next time."

There may be other reinforcers. Any planned extinction program must include an analysis of the behavior, the situation that provokes the tantrums, and your response. Look carefully at all these factors for insight into what is maintaining the tantrums. The procedures for dealing with behavior, once we understand it, are straightforward. We must look for ways to deprive the child of reinforcement.

As we mentioned earlier, do not start any plan to extinguish your child's tantrum unless you are committed to seeing it through to the end. Be aware that the early stages of your attempt to regain control of your child's behavior may actually cause temper tantrums to become more frequent or more violent than those you have already seen. This should not alarm you. Attempts to stop well-established habits cause most of us to push a little harder to continue to get our way. This will probably occur with your child. If you know this in advance and understand the significance of the behavior, you will be able to plan your actions and see them through to a satisfactory conclusion.

We should add a few more words about ignoring temper tantrums. Ignoring a temper tantrum is a good idea. The problem is that it is difficult to do and does not work well in actual practice. The theory is fine. By ignoring a tantrum, you deprive a child of reinforcers. You give her neither what she wants nor the attention she seems to be seeking. However, even very young children know that if they lie on the living room rug kicking, screaming, and threatening to smash lamps and tear up furniture, you can hear them in the kitchen and will be affected by their behavior. Even going into another room and pretending disinterest in the screams and threats to dismantle portions of the house rarely works out well.

The most effective means of extinguishing a temper tantrum is to isolate a child, preferably in his own bedroom. Practical factors might make this difficult and we will discuss these factors further on, but here we will outline the steps required to implement this suggestion.

First, explain to your child one more time that there are new house rules. Point out that his tantrums are disruptive and upset everyone, including the child himself. At any time when he begins to fuss, ask him to go to his room and stay there until he has settled down on his own. He can then come out and rejoin the family.

Of course, this explanation itself is not going to make a bit of difference in your child's behavior. We only suggest it to signal that things are going to be different. Now, action is more important than talk.

You know best whether your child understands the rules. Most 2-year-olds can understand the rule you just read. They do not gain more understanding from a second explanation.

Too often, parents try to reason with their children or explain the importance of rules and their consequences during times of greatest turmoil. Consider your own experience. In the midst of a heated argument, how receptive are you to someone's explanation of why you are wrong and why you ought to change your behavior? Later, when you have calmed down, you might be receptive to the same arguments you would not listen to when you were angry or upset. The same ideas apply to managing your child. If you want to explain, do so later, not while you are implementing the isolation procedures. Let your actions speak for you.

We think it is important to tell a child that she must remain in her room only long enough to control her behavior. This may mean that she marches in screaming, does an immediate about-face, and walks back out. This advice may not work well with a child in the early stages of this procedure, but emphasize to your child the importance of gaining control of her own behavior. It is far more effective to emphasize a child's control of her own behavior rather than your control as a parent. Our goal is to get you out of the business of saying how long your child should spend in her room. She may be incapable of gaining control over her own impulsivity, but try.

The early stages.   Be certain that you have explained to your child what objectionable behavior is under consideration. Do not tell him that you are going to put him in his room when he is "bad." You will get nowhere if you tell him to "behave himself." Remember to make your descriptions of behavior as objective as possible. Let him know that raising his voice above a certain level, hitting his sister, throwing food at the kitchen table, or using offensive language are the behaviors you find objectionable. Keep in mind that we are working to change behavior, not attitudes or feelings. To return to our example, the next time a tantrum begins, send the child to his room. If he refuses to go, pick him up and carry him there, place him in his room, turn around, and close the door. Walk out. Do not explain anything. Do not wait for the behavior to escalate into a major tantrum.

Like most parents, you probably have developed a sixth sense for reading early protests and preliminary threats in order to determine whether an episode can be safely ignored or if it will be "one of the big ones." Forget those distinctions for the time being. Move swiftly. At the first sign of the behavior you want to extinguish, isolate the child in his room.

Now what? If your child is like most, he will not stay there. He will probably be 3 feet behind you, still screaming and fussing, as you walk out of his room. He may stay in his room for a few minutes, even settle down, only to come out and resume the same disruptive behavior a short while later.

Follow through. Do it again. Take him back to his room.

How long do you keep doing this? As long as necessary. If your child refuses to stay in his room, lock the door. If the door has no lock, go to a hardware store, get a small hook and eye, and latch the door from the outside.

Leave the light on. Assure the child in a calm, quiet way that you will be outside, and that he can come out as soon as he settles down.

The lock upsets many children. Reassure your child calmly, but only once, that you will stop using the lock as soon as he gets sufficient control of his behavior to stay in his room with the door unlatched. If your child is loudly screaming about the lock, it may seem as if he does not hear your reassurance. Say it only once anyway. Do not argue. Save your logical approach for a time when you both are calm. The use of the lock is temporary and rarely necessary for more than a few days. After your child has settled down, remind him again, but only once, that you will use the lock only as long as he refuses to remain in his room.

These procedures should be sufficient to eliminate most tantrums. A few children, however, will carry on to such an extent that new questions are raised. For example, how long do you allow a child to scream and kick in a violent rage in her room? The answer is simple: until she settles down. In some instances this can be 4, 5, or even 6 to 8 hours. That is unusual, but if you hang on the first time for 8 hours, you will never have to do it again.

Another question that arises is, "What do we do if he starts destroying things in his room?" You know your child. It might be a good idea to remove most things from your child's room while you are working to get the tantrums under control. It probably will be for no more than 2 weeks. You might want to put the dresser in the hall, remove items from any wall shelves, and possibly even clean out his closet. Alternatively, leave everything in his room and let him make as big a mess as he can. Do not clean it up. When the behavior is under control in a few days, have your child straighten up for himself—with your assistance.

Some children become so agitated that we fear for their safety. A child can jump off her bed in a rage and hit her head against the corner of a dresser. Windows can be broken. Light fixtures can be shattered. By now you are probably shaking your head and saying, "Not me. I'm not putting the family through that."

You can see why we warned you not to start procedures unless you are prepared to follow through to the end. Perhaps furniture should be removed from the child's room. Depending on your child, it may be safest to leave only a mattress in the room.

Many parents stand outside a child's door listening to the quiet that descends after hours of vigorous, violent protest, wondering fearfully what has happened. Has he hurt himself? Has he stopped breathing? Is he still there? You might find it helpful to drill a small observation hole through the door so that you can unobtrusively peek into his bedroom to reassure yourself that he is safe. Drilling an observation hole in the door and fastening extra locks to the outside may destroy the door. Only you can decide whether the cost of a new door is a fair price to pay for control of your child's tantrum behavior.

Children do not hurt themselves physically or mentally from temper tantrums. However, if your child's behavior is especially difficult to control, it might be best for your child, and for your own peace of mind, to follow the behavior management program under the direction of either your family doctor or a psychologist. These doctors can reassure you about your child's response to your strict management, give guidance and support when your confidence flags, and deal with any angry or hostile feelings this program creates in your child. Temporarily, your child might become very angry with you. Nonetheless, this sort of anger can be managed easily and is far less destructive than the long-term feelings of hostility, alienation, and rejection that arise in families if the temper tantrums are allowed to persist.

It is not easy to listen to your child tell you that she hates you. In many ways, it is even more frightening when, in your own mind, you begin to think, I hate you too. These are normal responses to this kind of situation, but everyone will feel better if you talk them over with a professional.

The middle stage.   You should see substantial changes in the frequency and intensity of the tantrums within a few days. You will know when you are on the right track. In the middle stage of management you should be able to place more responsibility on your child. The lock on the door should no longer be necessary. He should be going to his room on his own when you send him.

Guard against premature feelings of success. You must remain very consistent. Continue to intervene quickly. Do not allow second chances. Do not tie yourself up with lengthy explanations. It is tempting to tell your child that he should understand all of the rules by now and you cannot understand why he does not comply when you first tell him to go to his room. If you have that discussion with him, you are undermining your own consistency and management program. If he has been going to his room regularly when instructed but hesitates one time, take his hand gently but firmly and move him along. If he leaves his room too quickly or begins the same argument again, you might have to lock him in another time or two.

Overall, continue at calm times to emphasize your child's control of her own behavior. At this point, you might also introduce a positive reinforcement program for hours or days when she has no tantrum. The same procedures we described earlier can be applied by the hour, the half-day, or the day for the child who is now going for longer and longer periods of time without temper tantrums.

The final stage.   There are only a few rules we can offer with certainty. One rule is this: If your child is tantrum-free for several weeks, you believe you have complete control of the problem, and you relax your vigilance, you can be assured that the temper tantrums will come right back, probably as strong as ever. You must be ready to return to the strictest application of the procedures discussed any time the temper tantrums reappear. Your child may try it again. Do not give the habit a chance to become reestablished.

5

Educational Planning and Management

Children with attention deficit–hyperactivity disorder often have problems in school. Many of the same difficulties they have at home interfere in the classroom and on the playground. They may also have trouble learning. By high school approximately 30% of students with ADHD have repeated a grade, and about 60% are from 1 to 2 years behind the expected achievement level.

The reasons for these learning problems include an inability to concentrate on lessons, different learning styles, and lack of self-confidence. In addition, many children with ADHD have learning disabilities. For example, visual-perception problems are common, and there is evidence that visual memory is not as good in children with ADHD as in their peers. Visual memory is the ability to see something and remember what it looks like. This skill is important in the early stages of learning to read.

Still unanswered is the question of whether children with ADHD have a special disability in these areas, or if their poor visual memory and learning problems can be explained entirely by their short attention span, impulsivity, and heightened distractibility. The best research to date suggests that difficulty paying attention is the primary classroom handicap problem for most youngsters with ADHD. A smaller, but significant, number of children with ADHD have additional learning disabilities that remain after the attentional problems have been dealt with.

LEARNING DISABILITIES AND THE CHILD WITH ADHD

A full discussion of learning disabilities is beyond the scope of this book, but some background will be useful. About 10% of all children, no matter what is done in the classroom, do not learn as well as would be expected based on their intellectual abilities. Youngsters with ADHD have a higher incidence of learning problems. Children with learning disabilities are not all the same. Learning disability is not a medical or psychological diagnosis; it is a problem description. Many different handicaps seem to cause a variety of learning disabilities.

A psychological diagnosis of learning disability may differ from the definition of learning disability used in your child's school. This is because each state department of education establishes the criteria for classifying a child as learning disabled in that state. There is, however, considerable agreement and uniformity, and most state educational departments' definitions of learning disability are based on national standards.

A learning disability is a disorder in one or more of the basic psychological processes involved in understanding or using language, spoken or written, which may show up as an imperfect ability to listen, think, speak, read, write, spell, or do mathematical calculations. The term *learning disability* includes such conditions as perceptual handicaps, brain injury, minimal brain dysfunction, dyslexia, and developmental aphasia. The term does not apply to children who have learning problems that are the result of visual, hearing, or motor handicaps; mental retardation; severe psychological disturbance; or cultural or economic disadvantage.

When a child has been taught in a way that is appropriate for his age and ability, but does not achieve as expected in one or more of the areas listed below, schools generally determine that the child has a learning disability and classify him as learning disabled. The areas of problem achievement are speaking, listening comprehension, writing, reading, mathematical calculation, and mathematical reasoning. We will discuss later the process school personnel use to decide whether or not a child is learning disabled.

Many children with learning problems also have attention problems. Some children also have visual-motor coordination problems, perceptual problems, visual and auditory memory problems, and, frequently, clumsiness. This may interfere with penmanship and create frustration. Perceptual problems often show up as an inability to discriminate right from left and confusion of "b" with "d" or "p" with "q." Children with perceptual problems may write or copy figures and letters backward or upside down. Confusion of right and left is a normal part of development for 5-year-old and many 6-year-old children, but it is cause for concern beyond this age.

SPECIAL EDUCATION PROCEDURES

Every school district has guidelines for determining whether a child has a learning disability. In all cases, the determination of disability is based on a comprehensive evaluation by a multidisciplinary team. The members of this team may differ from school district to school district, but the membership is spelled out and steps by which the diagnosis and evaluations are undertaken are written down. You can get this information from your school district.

The evaluation team always includes a contribution by a child's regular teacher. If, for some reason, the child is not in school, a regular classroom teacher qualified to teach a child of the same age is usually included. In addition, the multidisciplinary team has at least one person who is qualified to conduct individual diagnostic examinations of children, such as a school psychologist, a teacher focusing on speech and language impairments, or some other specialist. School social workers frequently assist in gathering information. In the case of older children, a school counselor, an administrator, and a variety of classroom teachers may contribute.

When a learning impairment is suspected, permission from parents is usually sought to allow members of this specialized multidisciplinary team to undertake the evaluation. After completing their testing and observations, the team members meet with parents, a procedure required by law in all states. A specialized instructional plan, often called an Individualized Education Plan, is then formulated. The plan includes contributions by all people who are familiar with the child. This includes parents, and in the case of older children, often the contribution of the children themselves.

If there is agreement between home and school, the program is implemented with appropriate follow-up and evaluation to determine the program's success. Subsequent meetings of the planning committee are held whenever necessary, particularly when any program change is made. If parents and school personnel cannot agree, every state provides, *by law*, guidelines that describe the parents' right to appeal and right to hearings before appropriate educational and legal agencies.

In most states a child is not eligible for special education help solely because of ADHD. The majority of children with ADHD, when they are certified as special education students, are classified as either learning disabled or emotionally disturbed. In many cases the diagnosis of learning disability or emotional disturbance is in error. As we noted earlier, the symptoms of ADHD are often misunderstood or misinterpreted. For some children, this error is fortunate because the child will get special help that would otherwise be denied. For others, failure to recognize ADHD and its relationship to learning and behavioral problems creates additional hardship for the child.

One of the most difficult cases occurs when the child's learning or behavior is affected by ADHD, but at a level that is not severe enough to be assigned to special education. Unfortunately, as the child gets older, the learning handicap and behavioral problems typically become more severe. By the time a child does meet the special education placement criteria, time has been wasted and the child's psychological problems have become worse.

TWO CASES OF MISDIAGNOSIS

Many children with ADHD do have learning disabilities and emotional disturbances. It is often difficult to determine the precise nature of the relationship between learning and emotional problems and ADHD. A child may not concentrate in school because he is anxious. A child with a learning disability who finds schoolwork difficult may become nervous and seem inattentive or disinterested in the work. It may be hard to decide what came first and to determine cause and effect.

Children with ADHD often require special help that is available only in a special education class. Sometimes ADHD is misdiagnosed and a child is incorrectly placed in a special class. At other times, a child with ADHD may need special class placement but is not eligible according to strict school regulations. Many youngsters with ADHD require nothing more than modest adjustments in their school program, whereas others require more extensive care; it depends on the individual case.

Following are two case studies describing common errors in diagnosis and conceptualization of school-related problems of children with ADHD.

Benjamin Collins

Benjamin Collins seemed to develop normally until he began kindergarten. Toward the end of the year, Ben's teacher told his parents that he was immature and recommended that he repeat the grade. She regarded him as immature because of his inability to settle down and follow instructions. She noted that he was responsive to discipline and did his work properly when she sat with him or stood over him. When he was left alone, he was mildly disruptive and could not finish assignments.

After Ben's second year in kindergarten, his teacher still had reservations about his behavior but thought he was ready for first grade. She knew that he was a bright boy and he seemed eager to learn. His report card noted that he had made a great deal of progress through the year, but continual effort in self-control and working independently would be required if he was to be successful.

Ben did not do as well in first grade as might be expected, based on his apparent level of intelligence. His parents regarded his teacher as strict but flexible, and, with some extra help, by the end of first grade everyone agreed that he could safely be promoted.

Three months into second grade Ben's teacher asked his parents to come to school for a conference. Ben was not doing the work. The teacher told Mr. and Mrs. Collins that Ben "could do it if he wanted to." She described him as immature and emotionally needy. He required a great deal of her attention. She suggested a psychological evaluation, suspecting that Benjamin might be psychologically disturbed.

Mr. and Mrs. Collins were upset, of course. They regarded themselves as capable parents, but after $3\frac{1}{2}$ years of frustration with Benjamin's behavior, they no longer felt as confident as they once did. They were especially troubled by the suggestion that their son demanded a great deal of attention. They questioned his teacher carefully. The only evidence in support of this idea was that when she gave Benjamin attention by working with him alone, he did satisfactorily. Without special attention, he did poorly. On this basis, she concluded that he must either need attention or feel very insecure.

The matter of Benjamin's insecurity was most troubling to his parents. If Benjamin was insecure, it could only mean that he did not feel loved, and they were failing as parents.

School specialists and Benjamin's pediatrician were consulted. The school social worker and psychologist recommended that Ben be classified as emotionally disturbed and placed in a special education class.

After $3\frac{1}{2}$ years in school, Ben had been labeled immature, insecure, possessed of a bad attitude toward school, unmotivated, possibly learning disabled, and psychologically disturbed.

They were all wrong!

Ben had ADHD. Fortunately, the class for emotionally disturbed children where Ben was placed had a teacher who recognized the zebra's hoofbeats and urged Mr. and Mrs. Collins to have Benjamin evaluated by a psychologist knowledgeable about ADHD.

Unfortunately, after years of frustration and failure, Benjamin did have the beginnings of some psychological problems that required additional treatment. After treatment with medication he returned to a regular classroom and, after another year of remedial help, he was able to do satisfactorily in a regular class where his achievement and behavior were no longer of concern.

Benjamin was lucky. Although he was 9 years old before an alert teacher recognized the symptoms of ADHD, the problem was diagnosed early enough so that something could be done to help. The psychological and schoolwork problems Benjamin did develop were mild enough to be treatable within a short time.

Unfortunately, Benjamin's 4 frustrating years of repeated failure, misguided efforts to help by teachers, and the continual discouragement that led to psychological problems were similar to what occurs with other children. As they get older, many children become disillusioned with school, and there is a high likelihood of dropping out and developing more serious psychological problems.

In the next case study you will see how a decision to certify a 9-year-old boy as eligible for special education, based on the mistaken notion that he had a learning disability, led to gratifying improvement in his school performance. The problem resulting from the misdiagnosis did not arise until he returned to a regular education program.

Matthew Richardson

Matthew Richardson was 9 years old when he first came to the attention of the school psychologist. He had repeated first grade. His third-grade teacher discussed his progress with Mr. and Mrs. Richardson and agreed to have the school psychologist test Matt. Despite the best efforts of Matthew's teachers, his reading level remained at a mid- to late first-grade level. His arithmetic achievement was better, but that too lagged a year behind what would be expected, based on his grade placement.

In contrast to Benjamin Collins, Matthew was a boy with a pleasant disposition and a cheerful, outgoing manner. He was troubled by the poor quality of his schoolwork, but it did not seem to affect his behavior in other areas of his life.

The school psychologist gave Matthew the *Wechsler Intelligence Scale for Children.* He scored considerably above average in most areas of the test with a Full Scale IQ of 114. Standardized achievement test results were consistent with teacher reports. Matthew read at the late first-grade level and did arithmetic at the second-grade level. History, the interview, and personality test results revealed no signs of significant psychological disturbance, although the psychologist's report said that Matthew was somewhat immature. That judgment was made because Matthew seemed irresponsible and did not follow through on instructions. At times, he would rather play than work.

The psychologist was able to rule out low intelligence and psychological disturbance as causes of Matthew's learning problem. It remained to be determined whether Matthew had a learning disability. As we noted earlier, there is considerable ambiguity in definitions of learning disabilities, and there appear to be many types. For Matthew, the school psychologist included tests of visual perception, visual-motor coordination, and perceptual integration in the test battery.

Matthew did poorly on several perceptual motor tests, especially the *Bender Visual Motor Gestalt Test* and the *Beery Developmental Test of Visual Motor Integration.* Both tests require a child to copy geometric shapes and designs. Matthew's reproductions were clumsy, poorly defined, and badly organized on the page.

A psychological or medical diagnosis is based on the absence of certain signs and symptoms and the presence of others. In Matthew's case the absence of signs of psychological disturbance or low intelligence allowed those possibilities to be ruled out. The presence of a perceptual problem, together with Matthew's long-term failure to benefit from regular classroom instruction and his poor achievement in relation to this intelligence led to the diagnosis of a learning disability.

A school committee consisting of Matthew's teacher, school psychologist, learning disability consultant, counselor, and principal met with Mr. and Mrs. Richardson and recommended that Matthew be certified as learning disabled and placed in a special education class, where he would get help from a specially trained teacher. Mr. and Mrs. Richardson were grateful for the opportunity to do something for their son and readily agreed. Matthew was also relieved and happy to get help for a problem that had frustrated him for so long.

Shortly after Matthew was placed in the special education program, Mrs. Richardson discussed the matter with Matthew's pediatrician. He agreed that the plan seemed sensible but suggested that Matthew be evaluated by a child psychologist at a nearby clinic for a second opinion. The child psychologist reviewed the test results obtained by the school psychologist. His attention was drawn to the reports of immature behavior, especially Matthew's disorganization, his occasional silliness, and descriptions of how he would rather play than work. He could hear the hoofbeats pounding in the distance. Horse's, he wondered, or possibly zebra's?

At an appointment with Matthew's parents, the psychologist reviewed Matthew's behavior and development in detail. He also asked the parents and Matthew's teachers to fill out several behavioral rating scales. The psychologist also reviewed Matthew's school records, including his report cards, school papers kept by his mother, and anecdotal materials maintained by the school in Matthew's permanent record. The words "short attention span" and "problems with self-control" appeared frequently. These problems were normally interpreted by Matthew's teachers as reflections of immaturity rather than as signals that something else might be wrong.

Based on this careful appraisal of Matthew's history, a diagnosis of ADHD was made. Matthew's ADHD was of only moderate severity. Neither his short attention span nor his impulse control problems seemed to create a behavioral problem, which would have been more likely to catch the attention of professionals and be diagnosed earlier. In Matthew's case, his disorder was expressed only as a learning problem; the significance of the behavior underlying the learning problem was not recognized.

Six weeks after Matthew began the special education program he was placed on Ritalin. Matthew did very well. He seemed to enjoy his new class and teacher, he appeared motivated, and his progress was gratifying. He completed the third grade in a self-contained, special education classroom and began fourth grade spending half the day in special education and half the day in a regular classroom.

At the end of fourth grade, his teachers prepared to wean him further from special education. In fifth grade, he spent two periods a day in the special classroom with a teacher he had now had for 3 years and who knew him well, and the remainder of the day in a regular fifth grade.

The school planning committee met with Mr. and Mrs. Richardson in April of Matthew's fifth-grade year and heard very positive reports from his general education and special education teachers. Matthew reportedly was achieving at grade level. Everyone at the meeting endorsed the decision to return Matthew to a regular education program full time for the sixth grade.

It was a decision made in ignorance and it was a disaster!

In early November, Matthew's counselor and one of his sixth-grade teachers asked for a meeting with Mr. and Mrs. Richardson. The quality of Matthew's schoolwork had deteriorated, and he had become belligerent and uncooperative. This came as a surprise to Matthew's parents because he showed no such behavior at home and had told them he was doing well. They were anticipating an excellent first report card.

Mr. and Mrs. Richardson agreed to work closely with the teachers and counselor to monitor Matthew's behavior and homework assignments. They all agreed to meet again shortly after the first of the year to evaluate Matthew's status.

By mid-January, Matthew's work had deteriorated further and his angry attitude about schoolwork spilled over at home. His parents were now arguing with him about incomplete assignments. It was a rare evening in the Richardson household when there was not at least one angry outburst leading to hurt feelings and tears. Toward the end of the month Matt refused to take his medicine.

What happened? What went wrong? Matthew seemed to have overcome his learning disability. He had been taking Ritalin. Yet he had gone from satisfactory achievement and a good disposition to failing work and a dreadful attitude.

The answer to the question of what went wrong lies in a better understanding of why Matthew had learning problems in the first place. This boy, now 12 years old, had been diagnosed as learning disabled when he was 9. Most of the decisions made about his educational program were based on the image of him as learning disabled. Matthew, however, never had a learning disability. At first, the error in diagnosis actually helped him because it enabled him to get special education help, which compensated to some extent for his ADHD. However, it was that same error in diagnosis that then led to the ill-fated decision to remove Matthew from special education and put him into a general education program full time.

Matthew had done well in special education, not because he had a learning disability and was being taught by a specially trained teacher, but because he had ADHD and responded well to the high degree of structure and support inherent in the learning disability special education classroom. He also did well because he benefited from the medicine, but even more importantly, because the special program he was in helped to compensate for his difficulties with attention span, distractibility, and disorganization.

This is where an accurate understanding of the problem is crucial. The special education program worked, but not for the reasons everyone thought. Matthew's learning disability was not being cured because he did not have a learning disability in the first place. The decision to return him to the regular classroom, based on the idea that his learning disability had been remediated, was completely off track. When the extra support, needed for only two periods a day, was taken from him in sixth grade, Matthew fell flat on his face.

Unfortunately, it was not a simple matter to rectify the error and put Matthew back into special education. By the time the full impact of the unfortunate decision was understood, it was March of Matthew's sixth-grade year, and he had spent 6 months becoming angry, frustrated, and discouraged. He was no longer 9 years old—he was almost 13, with all of the difficulties early adolescence brings. He was threatened and frightened by the poor quality of his schoolwork, which made him angrier. He vigorously resisted the suggested return to the special education class for several hours a day, insisting that he did not need help. He said that he could do the work if he wanted to; he just did not want to. No amount of logic or reasonable discussion would persuade him otherwise. He stopped taking all medicine.

Ultimately, the story of Matthew Richardson has a positive ending. Matthew was able to develop a good relationship with the clinical psychologist who originally examined him and who provided supportive psychological counseling. He helped Matthew understand the causes of his learning difficulties and his bad feelings about himself. By September of the following year, Matthew was again willing to take his medicine and accept two periods a day in the special education resource room. This provided sufficient support over the next several years for him to get his schoolwork back on track. Although he never obtained grades that might be expected based on his IQ level, he passed all courses and is still doing satisfactorily at the time of this writing.

This erroneous diagnosis of a learning disability reflects errors that occur every day. The definition of a learning disability requires that the learning problem not be caused by limited intelligence, faulty instruction, psychological disturbance, or social factors, such as a severely disrupted family. Those are the negatives that have to be ruled out.

The positive findings that allow a child to be certified as learning disabled include a variety of language and language processing disabilities and the perceptual problem Matthew was thought to display. Although solid evidence in Matthew's case ruled out other causes of learning problems, the only positive factor to support a diagnosis of learning disability was his poor performance on the perceptual tests. About half of all children labeled learning disabled have been so classified on the basis of perceptual or perceptual-motor problems.

Although they were given scant attention at the time because Matthew was doing well in special education class, test records in his file showed that the diagnosis of perceptual problems had been in error. Three weeks after Matthew began taking Ritalin, he was retested on several of the tests that were part of the school psychologist's initial test battery. Included were the *Bender Gestalt Test* and the *Beery Perceptual Development Test*. In both cases Matthew was taking Ritalin at the time of these tests and the quality of his performance was markedly improved over the initial testing. His improvement gains were far beyond expectations based solely on his previous practice of these designs. Results of this second administration showed no evidence of a perceptual problem.

To be certain, the psychologist tested Matthew again with the same tests several hours later in the day when the medicine had worn off. The results were almost identical to the first tests by the school psychologist.

The poor quality of drawings did not reflect a perceptual problem, a visual-motor integration problem, or any kind of coordination problem. Matthew's distractibility and impulsivity lay at the root. Poor performance on these tests often indicates a perceptual problem; poor-quality work may reflect other causes as well. In Matthew's case, clumsy drawings expressed the symptoms of ADHD. Listen carefully for the zebra's hoofbeats!

MANAGING THE CHILD IN SCHOOL

Treatment of learning problems must be based on an accurate assessment of the nature of the problem. Unfortunately, a lot of questionable remedial educational programs exist. Many are called "perceptual-motor training programs." These run the gamut from eye training exercises, through extensive tracing practice and copying of geometric figures, to the presentation of tactile, kinesthetic, auditory, and visual stimuli. Practice exercises like these do not seem to help children learn to read. They are a waste of time for children with ADHD who have learning problems. A joint statement prepared a number of years ago by the American Academy of Pediatrics, the American Academy of Ophthalmology and Otolaryngology, and the American Association of Ophthalmology stated: "No known scientific evidence supports the claims for improving the academic abilities of learning disabled or dyslexic children with treatment based solely on visual training (or) neurologic organizational training (balance board, perceptual training)."

Children with ADHD who have reading problems can be helped. A number of fairly sophisticated remedial programs are effective, although they are expensive in terms of time. It is vitally important to resist the temptation to look for shortcuts. Consideration must be given to the reading level of the child. If a 10-year-old child has the reading skills of a first-grade student, teachers and parents are often impatient and do not want to start remediation at the first-grade level. This is necessary, however. Impatience and reliance on shortcuts account for many of the failures of remedial reading programs.

This is particularly important for children with ADHD, who require careful, meticulous attention to detail and organization. The best remedial reading program for most children with ADHD who have learning problems is a rigorous emphasis on phonics and the use of a great deal of overlearning at each level. This includes allowing absolutely no progression to the next stage before a child has mastered each skill level.

These techniques are developed from learning principles for children with ADHD.

Most children with ADHD can be taught effectively in a regular classroom. With supplemental or remedial help, they can usually remain in a regular school program. If the problem is recognized and treated early, achievement problems can be held to a minimum. When the ADHD diagnosis is neglected and children are placed in special classes for students with other handicaps, the children with ADHD receive some of the extra help they need, such as a high degree of structure and organization and more individual instruction. Placement in special classes then confirms the erroneous diagnosis that first led to placement. Thus, as in Matt's case, appropriate medical and psychological care is further delayed, and the chance to be educated in a regular school classroom is denied.

School is a source of much frustration for children with ADHD (and for their parents and teachers). But understanding ADHD helps everyone. Share this book with your child's teacher. Remember that problems in the classroom and in social relationships are chronic. They will not be cured and the symptoms will not be totally eliminated. Adults must learn to deal with disruptions in the classroom and in their personal lives. This does not mean that children with ADHD should be allowed to run free or intrude on other people. It does not mean that the school or family must compromise expectations and values. It does mean taking a more relaxed, more accepting, and more understanding approach to many learning and behavioral characteristics.

Too many children with ADHD carry home exercise books and worksheets with abusive, critical, insensitive comments from teachers. A child with ADHD is not helped by a teacher who scrawls across the top of a clumsily done arithmetic worksheet, "John is going to have to improve his attitude and his work habits or he'll find himself in summer school." Labeling children as "immature," "lazy," or "attention-seeking" without considering what underlies the behavior is a main cause of the poor opinion many youngsters with ADHD and learning disabilities have about themselves.

Faced with this sort of criticism, and feeling helpless about making the work better, a child with ADHD has little choice. Two avenues are open to her. To protect what fragile self-esteem she still has, she may try to convince herself that school is unimportant and people with high expectations for her are either irrelevant or her enemies. She may reject school values altogether.

Many of these children then try to bolster their fragile self-esteem by looking for status in other ways. Sadly, the things they do to make themselves feel better, such as joining delinquent gangs, committing acts of vandalism, using marijuana, smoking cigarettes, getting drunk, skipping school, or performing other acts of rebellion, get them into further trouble. This, then, causes more rejection by the very people whose acceptance they so desperately want. A vicious cycle is perpetuated.

The other route the disillusioned, discouraged youngster with ADHD takes when he cannot satisfy his parents and teachers is that of withdrawing and becoming apathetic and disinterested. He differs from the child who chooses the path of rebellion by letting you see the feelings of hurt, discouragement, and anxiety. He is not, however, better off because he openly shows his feelings. The same downward spiral continues, until, with luck, it is interrupted by appropriate medical, psychological, and educational attention.

Research by psychologists at the University of California offers dramatic evidence of the interaction between the behavior of children with ADHD and their teachers. The researchers studied the behavior of teachers toward a group of hyperactive children, one-half of whom received Ritalin and one-half a placebo. The teachers did not know which children received each type of pill.

The teachers' behavior toward the children with ADHD on Ritalin changed markedly. They began to respond to them as they did to other children. There was no change in their behavior toward children receiving the placebo, however. With this latter group, teachers were more intense and controlling. They gave more orders, scolded more often, spoke more loudly and rapidly, and smiled less. Other researchers have demonstrated similar patterns in the parents of children with ADHD.

This is evidence of the many factors to be considered in evaluating and treating the child with ADHD. There is rarely a single cause for behavior. For each of us, even the youngest child, life is complex. To constantly remind ourselves of this complexity is essential to be most helpful to our children with ADHD.

Setting Goals

Helping a child with ADHD to follow rules, develop a sense of responsibility, and learn to control her own behavior requires careful attention to goal setting. When setting behavior standards for most children, it is usually possible to get by with a general idea of what you want. You must be more specific and explicit with a child who has ADHD. Recall our discussion in chapter 5 of the learning characteristics of children with ADHD. They must have clearly stated goals, and you must provide contingent reinforcement.

The teacher who wants a child to take home a book to complete an assignment may regard that as a single goal, but it is really several goals. One goal is to have the book arrive at the child's home. Another goal, which often is not made explicit, is to have the child remember the book in the first place and accept the responsibility for taking it home himself. If the goal is to get the book home, the teacher must separate that goal from the goal of having the child do it on his own. If the latter goal is not possible, and if the teacher fails to recognize this, the teacher may not take the necessary steps to attain the first goal—simply getting the book home.

The thoughtful teacher, with carefully worked-out goals, will make an extra effort to see that the student walks out carrying his book. It may be necessary to chase the child out the front door of the school and hand him his book. Another teacher might even stop at the child's house to drop off the book if it was left at school. Of course, there are limits to how far any teacher should be expected to go, but we use this example to emphasize that our goals must be clear-cut and our commitment to them firmly based on our knowledge about ADHD.

Once again, we are mindful of the fact that we must not encourage dependency or manipulation. Many children would like to be relieved of the responsibility for remembering books and supplies and rely on their teacher to help. All children can learn bad habits. If we are not careful, we may encourage dependency in the child with ADHD to the point where she looks to others to compensate for her handicap. Nonetheless, despite the dangers, frustration, and extra work inherent in our recommendations, we must never lose sight of the fact that ADHD is a significant handicap, which demands that a child be given special help. We must remember that a child's inability to stay organized or keep his mind on carrying his book home at the end of the day does not reflect immaturity, a bad attitude, or irresponsibility. It is a symptom of a physical disorder and requires compensatory help as would be true of a child with a more obvious handicap.

Another common practice provides an excellent illustration of the importance of clear goal setting for children with ADHD. A note sent home by the teacher often helps to organize a child's assignments, track homework and other projects, and provide a means for communication between teacher and parent. Parents can follow through and see that homework is done. Completed work gives the child a feeling of success and accomplishment, rather than another experience of failure.

The frequency of notes from the teacher to the parent and back should depend on your goal—what you expect to accomplish with the notes. If, for example, your goal is simply to keep informed about your child, a note every week or two should be sufficient. If the goal is to obtain parental support for a particular project or assignment, such as a book report or library research, the note can be sent home only when these special needs arise.

On the other hand, the most common reason for using notes is to ensure that a student keeps up with assignments, completes the homework, and turns it in. If this is your goal, a daily note is required. Only a daily note will ensure that work is done on a timely basis. We have seen many examples where a child brings home a note on Friday listing all incomplete assignments for the week. We cannot help but wonder about the goal for a once-a-week note system. Is the child expected to make up in two days all the work she found impossible to do in five days? If that is the goal, it seems unrealistic. How can we expect a child who cannot concentrate on her work long enough to complete it efficiently in five days to do the work in two?

It has been our experience that there is a strong punitive component, which is perhaps not explicit, in the minds of parents and teachers in cases where homework assignment notes are sent home weekly on Friday. It is like saying to the child, "Okay, if you don't want to do your work during the week, you can just sacrifice your weekend."

If we analyze this statement for the implied goal, it is not to help the child complete the work, but to punish him for not doing it. That is probably not what most parents and teachers intend, but it is what happens if you do not give careful attention to formulating a clear goal and to developing a plan leading to that goal.

Here we will limit our discussion to the issue of goal setting. In our present example, the goal should be to help the child complete as much of the schoolwork as possible.

Now, if our goal is to help a child finish schoolwork, notes must be sent every day. A clear-cut system has to be worked out between school and home. This is the only way we can realistically expect the job to get done. We will give a detailed plan for supervision of homework later in this chapter.

We are mindful that not all teachers, schools, or parents are willing or able to develop and maintain such a program. Many do it for a while and then become discouraged when inevitable complications occur; the program is then either discarded or allowed to lapse. There are no halfway measures that will yield halfway success. Not all children need such an elaborate program, but for the student who does, parents and teacher must provide for his needs or accept their share of the responsibility when the child fails.

It is easy to lose sight of your goals and, because of anger and frustration, allow your management techniques to become punitive. In the back of many minds is the recurring phrase, "She brought this on herself" to justify punishment or allowing a child to fall into painful situations that need not have occurred.

For example, Sarah, a hyperactive 5½-year-old kindergarten student, was put in the corner for acting up during recess. Can you guess the teacher's goal? We do not know, but it was probably some vaguely formulated goal about forcing Sarah to behave better. Now, if the teacher's goal was to frustrate and embarrass Sarah and to add to the peer-relation problems she had, the strategy worked well. The teacher knew that Sarah was hyperactive and was being treated with medication and psychological counseling. He should have known that putting her in the corner would have no effect at all on her behavior during recess. It would, if anything, make it worse.

To say, as Sarah's teacher did, that Sarah was given three chances and three warnings before she was put in the corner begs the issue of what the goals were. This treatment is still cruel and ineffective punishment.

For Sarah, recess, gym class, lunchtime, and other unstructured activities are fraught with peril. She becomes overexcited and finds it difficult to put restraints on her own behavior; her normal hyperactivity is exaggerated. This means that she requires greater supervision on the playground. It also means that the teacher will have to develop greater tolerance for Sarah's inability to stand quietly in line waiting her turn and more patience with her difficulty in settling down to quiet activities after a period of excitement and physical activity. However, it does not mean the teacher must tolerate significant disruption of the class or the activities of other children.

If Sarah cannot control her behavior with proper supervision and realistic expectations, it may be necessary to exclude her from some activities. Excluding Sarah from gym would not be pleasant for her. It would be another failure and would deprive her of an activity she enjoys. Nonetheless, if necessary, it could be done in a positive, constructive way by giving her an alternative activity that carries with it a sense of pride and accomplishment. Even at 5½ years of age, Sarah could be helped to understand that she has problems in unstructured situations, but that she is not being punished, humiliated, or rejected because of them. Rather, she is being protected from those problems and offered an alternative activity that she will enjoy.

This is not a perfect solution. It requires extra effort on the part of educational personnel and it cannot (and in fact, should not) be hidden from Sarah that this is a compromise solution in the face of a serious problem. Nonetheless, such a compromise is often necessary and would be consistent with our goals for a child such as Sarah. This solution would be preferable to daily punishment. We will return to the subject of goal setting and nonpunitive discipline in chapter 10.

Lack of Motivation

Motivation to do well in school, especially in young children, is misunderstood by many parents and teachers. "If only we could motivate him" is a phrase heard so often that it might lead us to consider lack of motivation the primary problem most teachers face.

An apparent lack of motivation is often misleading, however. Think about it for a moment. A young child in kindergarten or first grade is usually filled with enthusiasm for school. Teachers and parents praise him for clumsy artwork. His songs and the poems he recites find an enthusiastic and uncritical audience of parents and grandparents. How could any child fail to respond positively.

When we encounter children in early elementary grades who appear to lack motivation, our ears perk up and we listen for the sounds of the zebra's hoofbeats. Their *apparent* lack of motivation has nothing to do with motivation in most cases. After all, how do we decide that a child is not motivated? We see him fail to complete his assignments or not follow through on tasks. A child may also tell us that he does not like school, but such complaints rarely occur until after the child has already experienced frustration and failure.

We do not measure motivation itself; instead, we assess it indirectly. We infer its presence or absence on the basis of what a child does. When we observe the child's failure to complete schoolwork, it looks as though she is not motivated. Failure to complete work is, of course, often the result of a short attention span, distractibility, and other symptoms of ADHD.

Again, we see how easy it is for a mistaken conclusion to lead parents and educators in the wrong direction. If a child's failure to finish schoolwork is regarded as a motivational problem, efforts will be directed toward motivating him. But the goal will be wrong. Perhaps behavior modification or reward programs will be instituted. Punishment or withdrawal of privileges will be used as an incentive. In the long run, these will not do much good. In fact, treating a child with ADHD this way will breed resentment, frustration, and further failure. Parents and teachers will also experience increased frustration because their plans are unsuccessful. At times, these feelings may lead to rejection of the child. Punishment should play only a minor role in discipline of a child with ADHD. Parents and teachers must be cautious to avoid punishing a child for behavior that is a result of something he cannot help.

Patterns of punishment based on lack of understanding of ADHD symptoms usually start early in a child's life but become more of a problem when school starts. Adults then begin to search for ways to force the child to complete schoolwork. Unfortunately, while all the inappropriate and harmful procedures are being used to change the child's behavior, the underlying problem, ADHD, is typically neglected.

When a teacher encounters behavior that appears to reflect lack of motivation, he or she should not ask, "How can we motivate this child?" That question will lead nowhere. A different question should be asked: "What is it that interferes with the child's motivation?" This question will lead the teacher to consider a wide range of possibilities and to find more constructive solutions.

ADHD is not the only problem interfering with a child's performance in school that looks like lack of motivation. Learning disabilities, limited intelligence, anxiety, depression, family problems, and a host of other physical and psychological disorders also make a child appear unmotivated. ADHD is one of the most common causes, however, and because of its chronicity, it is relatively easy to distinguish ADHD from an apparent lack of motivation resulting from other causes.

In older children it may be more difficult to separate lack of motivation from problems that interfere with motivation. By the time a child is in sixth or seventh grade, and especially by the time she reaches high school, motivation does play an important role in the quality of the child's schoolwork. Even here, however, the teacher should keep ADHD in mind, and it is still worth asking the question, "What interfered with motivation?" Often it was our failure to recognize ADHD or other problems at an earlier age.

ADHD and Level of Intelligence

There is no relationship between intelligence and ADHD. Our experience suggests that there are an equal number of children with ADHD among the mentally retarded and the intellectually gifted.

There are problems in recognizing ADHD in children of especially low or high ability, but the principles of diagnosis and management remain the same. As children get older, they can sit still for longer periods, pay attention better, and control their own behavior. Since children of limited intelligence develop more slowly than those with normal intelligence, they may be more active or impulsive or have a shorter attention span than other children their age. Careful attention must be given to differentiating between symptoms suggestive of ADHD and behaviors resulting from a child's limited intelligence and slower development.

Very bright children may learn ways to compensate for some ADHD symptoms. They also may offer creative, but incorrect, explanations for the difficulty they have completing schoolwork. Parents, teachers, and doctors are often misled at first. In addition, there is a folk myth that bright children, if they are bored, will behave in a way similar to that of a child with ADHD. While it is certainly true that many bright children become bored with a regular school curriculum, boredom does not yield the pervasive, long-standing pattern of symptoms we see in ADHD. In fact, if an enriched program does not help a bright child complete assignments and control his classroom behavior better, it is an indication that the child might have ADHD, and the diagnosis should be pursued with professional help.

Homework

Homework causes problems in many families. Years after ADHD has been diagnosed, parents may still not understand or accept the impact of ADHD on a child's ability to fully complete schoolwork. For the younger child, homework consists of unfinished work as well as regular assignments. These often include projects to be completed over a period of days or weeks. Longer projects are especially difficult. The extended period of time adds to the lack of structure, which results in more unfinished assignments.

Homework, of course, is important in and of itself, but it takes on even greater significance in families where children have ADHD because it is often the major source of conflict. For example, we frequently have parents tell us that the worst problem they have to deal with is lying. Most of these lies are over schoolwork. Parents ask a child if she has homework, or how things are going at school. The child lies and says that she has no homework and school is going just fine. Later, teachers' notes, progress reports, and report cards tell the true story, and arguments erupt over honesty and trust.

There are other ways in which homework causes trouble in family relationships. For example, parents may try to control a child's completion of homework by withholding an allowance, restricting certain privileges, or, for the older child, denying access to the family car. Heated arguments then develop about these issues. Family members feel overwhelmed by a myriad of problems. Everyone forgets that much of the anger and bitterness can be traced back to the cause of the original problem in getting schoolwork done—ADHD.

We must learn to ask, "How can we help this child get the work done?" There are several reasons children with ADHD fail to complete schoolwork. The first is a direct expression of the disorder's symptoms. Schoolwork is not finished because the child finds it difficult to concentrate and organize himself. Second, children become angry and resentful over parents' efforts to control their behavior, especially if those efforts are punitive and consist of grounding or withdrawal of privileges. In these circumstances, children readily develop negative attitudes toward schoolwork and dig in their heels to resist.

A third reason reflects the lack of confidence and fear of failure that develop. If a child faces continual criticism, poor grades, and the feeling that she is not smart enough to get the job done, she will give up. Why try if it never seems to go right? What adult would be willing to continue at a job filled with failure and criticism every day?

We have found that the main mistake parents and teachers make is to confuse these three causes of school-related problems. This leads to misdirected efforts to solve the problem. Usually it is easy to recognize a bad attitude or resistance to schoolwork, but it is much more difficult to see how that bad attitude began. So parents and teachers may be tempted to view incomplete schoolwork as a discipline problem. For a child with ADHD, that is a serious error.

There is only one way to help a child with ADHD complete schoolwork. Note the word "help." This is not a discussion of how to force your child to complete homework—that cannot be done. Parents often ask, "How can we get our child to understand how important it is to do schoolwork and homework?" Do you really think that your child does not understand, or has not learned the importance of education? Of course the child has learned and understands. Keep in mind your goals and do not ask the wrong questions. Here the question is "How can we help the child get the work done?"

The steps to be followed are deceptively simple. Most parents will have already tried a similar technique. It is best if this procedure can be instituted and maintained from the very early days of a child's school career, but it can be put into practice at any stage. Simply stated, parents and teachers must offer the child their own ability to concentrate and organize things. They must substitute their greater frustration tolerance for the child's. They must compensate for his disability. This requires considerable cooperation between parent and school. Unfortunately, this cooperation is difficult to obtain at times.

Teachers should send a note home each day that outlines the work the child must complete. This makes quite a demand on a teacher's time, but there is no other way. The child is the messenger, but the teacher must accept responsibility for giving the child the message to be delivered.

Sadly, we often hear teachers say that they do not want to use the daily-note procedure because a child in, say, fifth or sixth grade is too old for that sort of thing. Other teachers argue that sending notes on a daily basis will never teach the child responsibility. Teachers who make such comments do not understand the nature of ADHD. The problem is not a matter of maturation, responsibility, or learning. It is based in a fundamental disability rooted in how a child's central nervous system works. Although ADHD is not a disease or illness, it is a reflection of the physiology and biochemistry of the child's nervous system. We should no more expect a child with ADHD to be "responsible," in the sense that she will accept all responsibility for completing her schoolwork, than we would expect a child who uses a wheelchair to accept the "responsibility" of walking on his own.

We have heard many teachers advise parents to withdraw their supervision or help with homework because of fear that the child would learn to rely on it. It is true that children with ADHD can become dependent. We must certainly remain vigilant to ensure that excessive dependency does not develop.

Nonetheless, we must remain equally cautious about allowing our fears of the child's dependency to serve as an excuse for not providing the needed help, support, and guidance. It is natural for you, after sitting with your child while he does his homework, or for his teacher, after supervising him one-on-one for a long period of time, to wonder when he will do his schoolwork by himself. We must, however, keep forever in mind that the child's inability to follow through, to stay organized, and to get things done by himself does not reflect irresponsibility, immaturity, or the lack of a skill he can learn. It is a handicap associated with ADHD that may require the compensatory help of teachers and parents throughout the child's school career.

As we develop a program for getting homework done, keep in mind that we are walking a thin line between pushing a child too hard to do things she simply cannot do because of ADHD and allowing her to get away with things any child would be happy to take advantage of. This latter threat is what makes teachers and parents leery and reluctant to adjust the child's curriculum; they fear that the child is getting away with something.

There is no precise way to determine exactly how much homework a particular child is able to do or exactly how long he can sit over a math textbook. If you sometimes require a little more than the child can do and at other times make a mistake and let him get away with a little less than he can do, you may get close to the truth. Little by little, you can understand with reasonable accuracy how much your child can actually handle.

We recognize that the child's difficulty with homework or other aspects of schoolwork reflects not only the ADHD but also all of the normal feelings and attitudes children bring to their school, as well as the discouragement and problems that come from coping with failure built up before the child's ADHD was recognized. One of the most important reasons for helping a child succeed with schoolwork is to show her that she is capable of doing the work and to create feelings of satisfaction and pride. Fear of failure is diminished when a child sees that she is not stupid and can do acceptable work on time. As fear of failure diminishes, conflict over schoolwork also is reduced. As a result, we see less passive aggressive behavior from children and less resistance in general to parents' requests.

Let us return to a step-by-step outline of how to use the daily-note system. Each day, the teacher must send home a note listing incomplete assignments or other work to be completed before the next day. Depending on the child's age, a time from $1/2$ hour to $1 1/2$ hours is set aside for a parent and child to work together on homework.

Children vary in how much supervision they need. Some will require little assistance, but others will need daily help throughout their school career. This is a major commitment for a parent, but there are no halfway measures. It is normally necessary for the child to do homework with the parent present, although some children will be able to work with only occasional supervision. Certain studies will require careful attention and cooperative effort between the child and parent. In other cases, a parent's presence at the table will be sufficient to provide the structure the child needs. Parents and teachers have to work out a communication system. It is best if each day a parent signs the homework note or writes comments before the child returns it to the teacher.

Adjust expectations with your child's teachers. See how much homework is realistic. Accept whatever work can be done during a specific amount of time. Many children with ADHD find it so difficult to concentrate or are so disorganized that it is impossible to complete the normal amount of schoolwork. Requirements will have to be adjusted.

It is not as difficult as it might first appear to learn how much your child can do. After you have worked at the kitchen table with your child for 3 to 4 weeks, you will have a good idea of whether he can work for 30 minutes or an hour. You will know when frustration begins to build. You will know when you are no longer accomplishing anything constructive and have reached a point leading to anger and tears. Of course, you can never be absolutely certain that your child is not feigning fatigue or manipulating you with anger. Some days you will probably press too hard, and some days you may allow your child to get away with his manipulations.

We never know exactly where that dividing line is. If you are careful and work consistently, you will develop a good feel for where this dividing line is.

Throughout this book we have urged parents and teachers to adjust their expectations and be flexible in managing children with ADHD. We have stressed the importance of not punishing a child for failure that results from a physical handicap. In the matter of homework, however, we urge you to develop very strict standards.

We would never suggest that you punish your child for a failing grade resulting from ADHD symptoms. We do think, however, that it is reasonable to use firm discipline to force your child to work on homework with you every night. The child who fails a spelling test after diligent study should not be punished. The child who refuses to practice spelling words the night before the test should face the consequences of her resistant behavior. Consequences can take the form of the loss of some privilege or other punishment. Be strict about forcing your child to work with you, but be accommodating in your response to grades and quality of schoolwork if the poor quality reflects the ADHD alone.

Many children will try to avoid homework. They will say that their teacher did not send a note or insist that no homework was assigned. Develop a foolproof plan so that opportunities for manipulation do not get out of hand. This is one reason for having a note sent every day—there can be no manipulation. When a parent or teacher is derelict in the responsibility of sending the note back and forth, children will often jump at the opportunity to use this adult lapse. On subsequent occasions, they may report that the teacher forgot or thought no note was necessary or that their mother did not sign the card this day.

We suggest that parents try to have a second set of schoolbooks at home. These may be old editions from the school or library. Sometimes it is possible to buy the books from a publisher. Even if actual textbooks and workbooks are not available, there are many items that are commercially available. We want to make sure that the child cannot avoid schoolwork. This is not a matter of punishment or discipline. It is an effort to protect the child from himself. A child tempted to lie his way out of a problem who is prevented from doing so is also prevented from having one more negative experience.

It is usually sufficient to tell children that they are expected to spend a certain amount of time on homework each evening. Although the teacher must be willing to supervise young children, older children typically can remember their books. We have found it effective never to allow the child to use the excuse that she left her books at school. When a child tries this excuse, we recommend that you use the duplicate set of books and increase the amount of schoolwork time for that one evening. Make the increase modest—add 10 or 15 minutes. The important message to send is that there is no way to avoid the responsibility and if she tries, she winds up in worse circumstances.

A program like this can be effective for children of any age. It is more complicated and difficult to implement in junior and senior high school because more teachers are involved. Often the child's counselor or special education teacher must accept responsibility for coordinating this system. Also, older children usually resist more.

Be cautious. Although the idea is simple, this is a difficult program to implement. The plan demands daily attention over a period of months and even years. As a consequence, it is easy to begin to wonder whether it is all worth it. Your vigilance may lapse because of the tedium or frequent conflict with your child.

The system may work well for a while. As long as it is working, parents and teachers may relax and not be as diligent in maintaining every detail. This often accounts for failure. ADHD is a chronic problem; it goes on and on. The necessary steps to help the child with ADHD must also go on and on, although there may be times in a child's life when such a strict system will not be necessary.

We want to highlight one other element inherent in this system. This supervision system distinguishes between the necessary adjustments in expectations for the child with ADHD and those requirements necessary to teach the child responsibility and self-reliance. Our goals with this system are to get as much work done as possible and to teach the child to make an effort and stick to it. Using the note system, we can accomplish both goals without being punitive.

COOPERATION BETWEEN HOME AND SCHOOL

Children learn best when their education is a cooperative effort between home and school. Because children with learning disabilities and ADHD encounter so much frustration and failure, parents often feel a great deal of disillusionment and dissatisfaction with the way their child is managed in school. Teachers, too, become frustrated and discouraged. Beware the trap of blaming the school for your child's difficulty. Over the years, we have worked with teachers, educational specialists, and administrators in countless schools in dozens of school districts. As we have previously noted, errors in instruction and child management may creep into your school's work with your child, and occasionally you will find teachers who are inefficient or ineffective, but there are also brilliant, gifted, and dedicated teachers to balance the teachers of questionable value. Time and again, we have been impressed with the sincerity and concern of teachers. It is rare to encounter a teacher who does not care or who takes his or her responsibility to your children superficially or indifferently. Bear in mind that teachers, too, suffer the same frustration you have experienced from dealing with a problem that goes on and on. Most of them continue to teach your children with as much enthusiasm and commitment as they did the very first day.

Given this frustration, parents and teachers often wind up blaming each other. Misunderstandings arise because of failure to understand the chronic, long-term nature of the problem or the subtle handicaps of the child with ADHD.

We can offer no simple guidelines to eliminate this problem. It will remain a problem as long as children have learning disabilities and ADHD. The goal of every parent and teacher should be to keep these sensitive issues in mind and to realize that when problems arise between home and school, they must be dealt with in a constructive way, rather than in a manner that emphasizes blame and assignment of responsibility for failure. Schools and parents work better as collaborators than as adversaries.

There are occasions when legitimate differences of opinion arise between parents and special education personnel. Special education laws in every state clearly define parents' rights. Parents can take steps to ask for a hearing or to appeal educational decisions with which they disagree. Nonetheless, legal steps are necessary in only a small fraction of cases. In most instances, parents and school personnel can work together to provide an optimum learning experience for the child with a learning problem.

6

Maintaining and Enhancing Self-Esteem

Lack of confidence, low self-esteem, and fear of failure are common problems for people with attention deficit–hyperactivity disorder. In their long-term follow-up study, *Hyperactive Children Grown Up* (1986), Gabriella Weiss and Lillian Hechtman noted that problems with self-esteem were the most common psychological difficulties of adults who had been diagnosed earlier as hyperactive. These observations have led educators, parents, and other professionals to place a high priority on finding ways to protect the self-esteem of children with ADHD.

Parents and teachers can do many things to help children feel better about themselves. Most of these ideas reflect simple common sense and do not require extensive effort. We will describe these suggestions in the following pages, but first let us review briefly how a child's self-image develops.

Self-concept has its roots in the earliest weeks of life when infants begin to differentiate between the self and the world around them. Gradually, infants learn that they are separate from the other things and people that make up their environment. Many parents watch with fascination as the baby is first startled, and then captivated, by the movement of his own hand. The child seems unable to tell what that oddly shaped structure is. He looks at it, studies it, and may even talk to it. The informed observer knows that much of that exploration in the early months of life is an effort to determine where the self stops and the rest of the world begins.

By learning to make these distinctions, children find out who and what they are. This is the first step in the development of an inner self-awareness, a psychological self-image that is the basis of the child's self-concept. It is the self-concept that we often equate with a child's level of self-esteem.

As children grow older, they develop an awareness of their inner selves. They discover that they have a unique personality different from everyone else's. Just as they have learned that their body is their own and separate from those of the other people and other things that make up their world, they also learn that their personality is their own.

Children learn at an astonishing rate. In only days, or even hours, after an infant discovers her own voice, she figures out how to control it and how to cry louder if she does not receive the attention she wants. By 10 months, a child probably will know that an image in a mirror is not another baby but a reflection of his own face. Children are fascinated by themselves and by comparisons with brothers, sisters, and parents. As they grow older, most children love to talk about themselves and to hear stories about what they were like and what they did when they were younger. Little by little, through the preschool years and into adulthood, children formulate an integrated idea of who they are.

As children grow, they look to certain people as models. Some models are more important than others as influences on the child's self-concept. Children's primary models are their parents, but later they have many more people to choose from. At ages 4 and 5 they begin to model the behavior of people outside their family; when they begin school they look toward favorite teachers as models. These models, in turn, have a strong influence on the developing child's self-concept. A capable, self-confident parent with whom the child can identify helps the child feel safe in his parents' protection and makes him confident that he will be able to manage his life competently.

Developmental psychologists often describe the establishment of an identity as a major task of adolescence. Adolescents must begin the final separation from their parents to become autonomous young adults. Accordingly, young teenagers may define themselves in speech and dress in a way that indicates clearly to everyone that they are no longer extensions of their parents. Clothes, speech, and behavior are intended to signal that they have pulled away from their identification with their parents. As people approach the later stages of adolescence, however, defining themselves simply as who they are *not* must give way to a coherent, comprehensive inner view of who they *are*. This final stage of self-definition establishes the foundation for the young adult to establish a mature relationship with a member of the opposite sex.

At every step of this often complex, but normal, process, children have experiences that teach them the value parents, friends, teachers, and society place on them. In most cases, a child who perceives himself as valued or important will develop a positive self-image. The child who is made to feel devalued by failure, rejection, and criticism, a common experience for children with ADHD, will acquire a negative self-image.

Self-concept changes with time; it does not stop changing when a person becomes an adult. A healthy self-concept grows more complete and more complex. A weak or poor self-concept may become more constricted and less flexible as a child withdraws more into herself. The self-image is diminished.

Each person has a public and a private self. People may allow others to see their public face, but some hide elements of their private self even from themselves. We should not expect a person to reveal his innermost thoughts to strangers, but, at times, a person's inner self is such an abundant source of bad feelings that it may inhibit or stunt his emotional growth. In such circumstances, he may be reluctant to examine how he feels about himself.

Each person also has an idea of her ideal self, the person she would like to be. It is mentally healthy to aspire to certain standards. There is also nothing wrong with recognizing that, in some areas, it may be impossible to reach the ideal. For many people with a poor self-concept, the gap between how they view themselves and what they would like to be is so great that it causes psychological distress. In such cases, children or adults may give up in despair of meeting the ideal. They may deliberately give way to their negative aspects and say, "If I can't be the wonderful person I want to be, I might as well let people see how rotten I can be."

In our practice, we often encounter people with unrealistic ideal self-concepts. Such individuals, whether children or adults, seem to demand perfection of themselves. They always want to win, always must be right, and may have a catastrophic reaction to failure. At times, their behavior puzzles us because it seems senseless. Why be concerned with winning every time or with always being right?

To answer that question, we must first understand that people who are obsessed with winning and intolerant of a reasonable amount of failure do not really have high standards for themselves. Rather, these individuals usually have such poor self-concepts, and are so fearful of failure, that they try constantly to secure a never-ending supply of positive experiences. These successes act as reassurance that the person is indeed adequate. A sure sign of a vulnerable or poor self-concept in a child is a need to win and an inability to tolerate criticism.

Many factors influence self-concept. Even a healthy self-image may be vulnerable to occasional challenges. The middle-aged woman who has remained at home to care for her children may question her value when her children are grown and leave home. The worker who loses his job, through no fault of his own, cannot help suffering a crisis of self-confidence. Nonetheless, the person with a positive self-concept and a healthy personality can face these experiences and cope with them successfully.

A person's self-image may be rewarding or punishing. People who behave consistently with their self-image feel pleased with themselves; this feeling is rewarding. The girl who considers herself a good musician will be praised by other musicians and by her parents after a good performance, but she also will gain satisfaction from having performed in a way that is consistent with her self-image. She will also feel some satisfaction and pleasure when she practices. A good self-concept normally continues to build in a positive way; a poor self-concept often grows worse as time passes.

Children with high self-esteem usually feel confident and self-assured; they are willing to risk failure or disapproval. Children and adults with low self-esteem, however, are often preoccupied with themselves. Interestingly, persons with a poor self-concept spend much more time thinking about themselves and their self-image than do those with a positive self-concept. As a result, persons with a poor self-image often withdraw in social situations or hesitate to attempt new tasks. Filled with self-doubt, they limit their own experiences, although those experiences might prove to them that they are more capable than they believe. Because they expect to fail, individuals with poor self-concepts frequently do not try very hard. Failure of effort leads to lack of success, which reinforces the sense of inadequacy. This cycle is destructive: Failure further reduces self-esteem and the reduction in self-esteem makes future failure more likely.

Research shows that firstborn and only children tend to have higher self-esteem than children who are born later. This finding may reflect the positive and undivided attention that firstborn and only children receive from their parents, although there is no conclusive supporting evidence. Another research finding is clear, however; physical attractiveness and other physical attributes do not significantly affect children's judgments of their own self-worth.

This last comment must be modified when we speak of adolescents. Their self-perceptions may be affected by how they feel about the physical changes taking place in their bodies. Many adolescents are temporarily dissatisfied with how they look. If you ask teenagers what their greatest concerns are, many will say skin problems, the color and quality of their hair, or lack of an athletic build or good figure. These concerns are mentioned much more frequently than worries about school or even social problems. As adolescents progress from junior high school to high school and from high school to college, they tend to see themselves in more favorable ways.

Self-concept may suffer when teenagers fear that their physical characteristics are unacceptable or different from those of their peers. For example, researchers have demonstrated that boys with slim, athletic builds have higher self-esteem than boys who see themselves as either too heavy or too thin. Girls display even more concern about their appearance and physical development. Adolescent girls in particular gain much of their self-esteem from others' opinions. For many adolescents, appearance is more important than any other personality attribute or ability.

Our self-image depends, at least in part, on the images we see reflected in the eyes of others. In the early stages of a child's life, parents are mirrors. If the parents indicate that they are happy with their children and consider them valuable, and if they demonstrate this commitment in a meaningful way, a high self-regard is created. On the other hand, parents who are indifferent to their children as infants and who also ignore them as they grow older give a straightforward message that the children are not especially valuable in the parents' eyes. It should not be surprising if a child raised this way grows up with a negative self-image.

It is worth mentioning that parents of children with high self-esteem tend to be reasonable and fair in discipline. They are emotionally stable and warm. These parents can usually get along with each other and have high self-esteem themselves.

It is not possible to trick your children into thinking that you have high regard for them when you do not. Fortunately, it is a rare parent who does not love and value his or her child, but having those feelings inside is not enough. You must demonstrate in word, and especially in deed, that you consider your child special. We certainly are not suggesting that you avoid criticizing or punishing your child when it is appropriate. Children learn to feel good about themselves not only because their parents accept them, but also because their parents set limits for them and teach them how to behave. You can show respect for your children by indicating that their ideas are important and respected. You should not, however, hesitate to let them know when they are wrong, nor should you be reluctant to set appropriate standards, expectations, and punishments.

The easiest way for a parent to show a child that he is valued is to spend time with the child. You can show respect for your youngsters or students by asking for and respecting their ideas. In this way you increase their feeling of self-importance. Children should be involved in family discussions and decision making. Such a practice helps them feel good about themselves; it shows that they are an integral part of the family and helps them to answer the question, "Who am I?"

In recent years it has become common practice for busy parents, who often both work outside the home, to emphasize "quality time" with their children. Many of these parents have sought reassurance that spending a brief period of quality time with their children is a substitute for longer periods together.

We are puzzled by the notion of quality time. No one seems to know exactly what it means. The quality of the time you spend with your children depends on the nature of your relationship, not on the activity. It is true, however, that time spent discussing your children's feelings and ideas is often quality time. Their opinions and reports of their activities are important. If you listen honestly and attentively, the time together should be regarded as quality time. Quality time may also be spent watching television together with your arm around your child. Exploring a museum or listening to classical music seem to be quality-time activities, but they are not if they are done in a rigid, self-conscious, or resentful way with one eye on the clock.

In fact, there is no substitute for spending time with your children. Even a passive activity, such as watching television or reading separately in the same room, may have value. You build your children's self-esteem by being with them, by showing that you want their company, and by your concern and interest in them.

The demands of modern life prevent many parents from spending large amounts of time with their children. Still, you must guard against the idea of quality time as an excuse to avoid a substantial commitment to your children. There is no substitute for attending your child's school concert, ball game, or scout activity. Explanations for your absence are not an alternative. No matter how logical, reasonable, and honest they are, they remain excuses. Your absence tells how you value your children more clearly than anything you might say. Usually, you cannot make up for your absence.

When you tell your children that business or other commitments make it difficult to spend time with them, you are saying that other things are more important and you prefer to be elsewhere. When you tell your children that they are of secondary importance in your life, you must not be surprised if they come to regard themselves as lacking value and develop flawed self-esteem.

THE SIGNIFICANCE OF SUCCESS AND FAILURE

Success and failure play a major role in influencing how we feel about ourselves, but the context in which these experiences occur is often more important than the success or the failure itself. The specific task is also important; some things matter more than others. A certain task or situation may be intimately related to how someone feels about herself but may have little significance for others.

Other people are often involved in our successes and failures. As observers or as participants, they may determine whether we succeed or fail. Who these people are, the nature of their relationships to us, and how we feel about them also influence how important they will be and how they will affect our self-concept.

We must keep this complex set of relationships in mind. Any of us can have a significant effect on other people's feelings through what we may consider only a minor experience. Similarly, events that are significant to us are not necessarily important to others. We must be alert to the effect of our behavior on others. Even with people we know well, we may not always understand why they react to certain experiences as they do. These ideas are important in considering how to avoid harming our children's self-esteem. They are also relevant to rebuilding the damaged self-concept of a child with ADHD.

Social psychologists obtained interesting information from a survey of married couples who were together for more than 10 years. The researchers were interested in individuals' responsiveness to their spouse's positive and negative comments about their appearance. Men and women responded in the same way; both were much more sensitive to their spouse's negative comments than to their positive comments. One woman said, "If my husband complains about my appearance, it makes me very upset. I don't even want to go and face other people if he is critical about my hair or my dress. On the other hand, I think if a stranger told me I didn't look good or criticized what I was wearing, it might make me feel bad for a moment, but I would just put it out of my mind and think that the person was a jerk."

The psychologists' findings and the woman's comment illustrate that it is easy to hurt the feelings of someone close to you. They also show why it can be difficult to make people feel good about themselves when offering praise.

Attribution theory, a related body of psychological knowledge, helps to explain these complex, seemingly contradictory ideas. Attribution theory stresses that an observer cannot understand another person's experience without knowing the meaning attributed to the experience. Generally your success or failure in something that is important to you will have a greater impact than in something that is unimportant. If you value someone, that person's opinion will be important. If you have no respect for an individual and consider him foolish, even severe criticism from the person will probably not hurt much. We must know how a person feels about a situation before we can judge the impact.

Consider two children facing a math test. One student has made a realistic assessment of her capabilities and recognizes herself to be a B student. She works hard and earns an A minus on the test. We might expect her to be very pleased. Another B student, who also has made a realistic appraisal of his abilities, has studied especially hard and is confident that he will make an A. He also earns an A minus. The first student did better than she expected; her A minus makes her feel good about herself. The second student did worse than he expected. Although he made a good grade, higher than his B average, he considered himself a failure because the grade did not meet his expectations. Without understanding this child's expectations and having some knowledge of attribution theory, we might wonder why his self-esteem suffered a blow even though he made an extremely good grade.

As noted above, it is not simply failure that causes self-esteem problems. We recently spoke to Edward a 22-year-old man with ADHD. After dropping out, he had returned to high school to complete his education. He was enrolled in several college courses and was already establishing himself in a business. We asked him why he thought he had been able to overcome the continual frustration and the frequent failure he had faced as a child and teenager.

Over the years, Edward said, he had learned that there was one fundamental difference between successful and unsuccessful people: Successful people were willing to do things others were not.

That statement made a lot of sense in terms of our own ideas about the healthy psychological development of the person with ADHD. It was especially meaningful when considered in relation to self-esteem. After all, what compels people to get up in the morning and face responsibilities they might not always enjoy, to work hard at a job when their natural inclination is to quit, or to take a risk that might lead to failure in school, at work, or in interpersonal relationships?

Successful people do these things regularly. This pattern of behavior distinguishes them from the less successful. These actions require a positive self-concept. An individual must have self-confidence and sufficiently high self-esteem to risk failure. She must also believe that there is a good chance of success from the extra effort.

As educators, parents, and psychologists, we face the task of maintaining the child's self-esteem, which is the foundation of a successful life. Children should be allowed to make decisions and occasionally to fail. Self-esteem does not result only from success; it also comes from a realistic knowledge of what one can and cannot do. We learn our strengths and limitations from both our successes and our failures. Parents and teachers who do not allow children to explore, experiment, and test their capabilities are as likely to cause self-doubt in the children as are parents and teachers who are careless and do not protect the children from excessive failure.

Failure can be a constructive learning experience. It teaches children realistic limits. They learn the limits of their capability and they can be confident of their abilities within those limits. Children and students should learn from their experiences and feel that they can do better next time.

Experiencing failure also removes fear of failure, because a child comes to realize that one can recover from an unsuccessful attempt or inadequate performance. From small day-to-day matters to major efforts in education, career, or family relationships, there is life after failure. Further opportunities exist. Failure usually does not mean rejection. The child's self-esteem does not suffer irreparable damage. Of course, we must constructively lead our children through their failures and not allow them to develop a fear of failure. When children fear failure, they are often afraid to try and develop self-doubt. Failure to try guarantees further failure and perpetuates the self-defeating cycle.

Be careful if you are tempted to hold back your children for their own protection. Help them to learn the decision-making process, which includes a careful assessment of the risks. If they realize that you have enough confidence in them to allow them to make decisions, they will have enough confidence in themselves to make those decisions and live with the consequences. If they are unsuccessful, they will not be afraid to return to you and let you witness their failure. They will look to you for help in learning from the experience and will try again.

PUTTING IDEAS TO WORK

We offer here some applications of these ideas and a few exercises to help your children or students build self-esteem. These exercises and suggestions include ways to help children feel more capable, significant, powerful, and worthy.

The ideas here are only illustrations of the many ways you can work to bolster a child's self-esteem. If you are creative and invest time, you can take other approaches to construct an almost unlimited number of exercises. You also can consult some good references if you want to make an extra effort in this area. (See the end of this chapter.) Most of the following examples have been adapted from these references.

Children differ dramatically in their ability to respond to and benefit from self-esteem exercises. If you encounter frustration in applying the material from this chapter, or in implementing a program outlined in one of the references, it may indicate that these procedures are not designed with the unique personality and temperament of your children in mind. Advice in self-help books and in books on interpersonal relationships is often presented in general terms. It must be refashioned for your specific circumstances. We must also remember that activities that work well for the average child in an ordinary classroom may not be appropriate for a child who is wounded, angry, and fearful in relationships, as are some children with ADHD.

Furthermore, children with ADHD may be unaware of their own behavior and the effects of that behavior on others. They may be less attuned to their own feelings and less aware of what goes on around them than children without this disorder. Of course, many other children with ADHD are acutely aware of other people and very sensitive to their own feelings; there are marked differences among children.

If we want to begin a program to boost a child's self-esteem, we must first ask whether some preliminary work is needed to make the child more aware of his feelings and behavior. Until the child is aware of what he is doing, and especially of how he feels, efforts to change his behavior and feelings will be ineffective.

Exercises to build self-esteem are valuable and can aid the child with ADHD. Remember, however, that self-concept is built through many years and countless experiences. Every experience has the potential to affect self-image. We can do very little in a brief time to make a major change in a person's self-esteem. The most significant impact on the self-esteem of a child with ADHD is made by the day-to-day responses of the important people in her life. There is no substitute for treating your child or student in a way that shows you care about her, value her as an individual, and respect her ideas and feelings.

Of course, there will never be a parent, teacher, or friend who offers only positive messages to a child with ADHD. Life is full of experiences, including some that are less than favorable. All of us, including those with ADHD, do many things that frustrate and anger others. Much of what we do is unsuccessful. Unfortunately, those with ADHD suffer more negative experiences than others. Most of us have occasionally been the object of someone's anger. These episodes, if properly understood as learning experiences, merely increase the complexity of our personalities and enrich our understanding of ourselves. It is failure and criticism that are harmful; they cause self-blame and lead to the destructive deterioration of self-regard.

We must try to avoid destructive, punitive criticism as we respond to the troublesome behavior of our children with ADHD. We also must help silence the self-criticism that develops so easily in these children.

From this perspective, let us examine some exercises for building self-esteem.

Learning About Self-Concept

You can do this brief exercise with friends or family members. Take a sheet of paper and write at the top, "Who am I?" Then see how many answers you can give.

People respond differently, but many begin by answering with their name. Others might first respond with their occupation; still others might define themselves by their role in the family, such as wife and mother or husband and father. Many people choose attributes such as good friend or loving child. The choices are limitless.

The order in which people write their answers may reflect something serious and important about how they see themselves or it may be nothing more than what occurs to them at the moment. The exercise, however, forces people to think of their own self-concept, the way they view themselves, and their definition of who they are.

Visualizing Your Self-Concept

Twenty-four brief sentences are listed below. Circle the sentences that express how you feel about yourself most of the time.

1. I am happy	2. I am sick	3. I am good
4. I am beautiful	5. I am a loser	6. I am a winner
7. I am a bore	8. I am a mess	9. I am calm and cool
10. I am successful	11. I am lovable	12. I am a failure
13. I am stupid	14. I am fine	15. I am sexy
16. I am okay	17. I am bad	18. I am clumsy
19. I am a gossip	20. I am neurotic	21. I am sad
22. I am smart	23. I am good at a job	24. I am friendly

How many of your circled sentences are you pleased with? Half of these sentences are positive and half are negative. Look at your responses in this light. What kind of self-picture do you see? That picture is a glimpse of your self-concept.

Do this exercise with other people in your family or with your students. You will all gain additional understanding of how you view yourselves.

Keeping a Journal

A journal is a practical, effective way of encouraging a child to pay attention to important experiences. The journal need not be detailed; certainly, it should not become another tedious assignment the child views with dread.

There are many ways to structure a journal. It is possible to make a brief entry each day, describing the best and worst things that happened. Children should be encouraged to describe their experiences briefly and to include what they did and how they felt.

Older children may be encouraged to record events about which they feel strongly. This assignment encourages more awareness of feelings. Once again, after the child records the event, he should note what he did and felt.

You can use your own creativity to tailor this exercise to the specific needs of your student or child; this is a starting point. Keeping a journal in itself does not have any effect on self-esteem. The child must be able to identify important experiences with the potential to affect self-esteem before anything can be done to change his feelings about himself.

The daily journal is not a private dairy. It should be started with the understanding that it will be reviewed every day or two with a parent or teacher. In some cases, this review will consist of only a brief discussion. In other cases, it may be beneficial to talk about the child's experiences in detail. In a few cases, it will be useful to narrow the focus to help the child understand what you want him to learn from the experience. You can encourage this focus by giving the child open-ended sentences such as "I learned that I . . ." or "I was surprised to find that I . . ." Use similar techniques to explore the child's reactions to other people.

The Personal Time Line

Give the child a long piece of paper. Holding it horizontally, ask her to draw a line about one-third of the way from the bottom from the left-hand margin to the right.

Beginning at the left, with birth, ask the child to write down important events and experiences in her life. You probably will need to stimulate the child's thinking by mentioning some of the more common experiences, such as learning to talk and walk. Children take delight in hearing stories about their infancy and early childhood; this is a good opportunity to bring out the baby book or sit down with a photo album and talk about the child and her early development.

Children will remember many of their experiences after age 5. They should be encouraged to record them. Although the personal time line exercise lasts only a few days, you should encourage the child to return to it from time to time. Suggest that she stop to think every once in a while; does she remember anything else important from the past year she would like to include? Be sure the child leaves plenty of room to fill in additional experiences.

If you later think of more experiences, bring them up and encourage the child to include them. The personal time line allows a child to become the center of attention, but not because of some behavior of the moment. Instead, the child is encouraged by seeing that her life has continuity and that she has been important all along.

A Success a Day

This exercise, like many others, can be done at home or in the classroom. It is appropriate for a single child or for a group.

Each day, ask the child to describe a success experience for that day. Children will initially find this task difficult, or they will be uncertain what you are asking for; they may describe an experience that is positive but not necessarily a success. It may be necessary for a parent, a teacher, a sibling, or a classmate to help a child recognize even the minor successes that occur every day.

The success-a-day exercise is valuable because it provides children with a feeling of accomplishment. It also forces them to focus on positive experiences that may pass unnoticed or may be lost in a cloud of negative experiences. It is especially helpful if children can experience success in areas where they are making special efforts, such as gaining increased self-control, doing better in schoolwork, or creating positive social interaction. Nonetheless, the main value of the success-a-day exercise comes from finding and recognizing positive experiences and accumulating many successes.

If possible, ask the child to record the success in a ledger divided by day, week, and month. If he is unable to write about the experience because of limited writing skills or age, do it for him.

At the end of the week and the month, review the success experiences and offer further praise and reinforcement. If there are patterns to the child's successes, point them out and discuss them. Be very careful, however, to keep this review positive. Do not use the child's successes to bring up failures or areas where the child could be working more constructively. There are other opportunities to guide a child to new areas of accomplishment; that is not the purpose of the success-a-day exercise. Nothing should be allowed to detract from the positive emphasis.

Above all, use your common sense. You need not be an expert in child development or education to see what is important to your children or students. Children want attention and they want to be special. You cannot love them too much or give them too much attention. Let children see your delight with their successes and your tolerance and forgiveness of their failures. Most of life is not a series of clear-cut successes or failures. Much of it is routine, filled with the day-to-day activities of learning, working, playing, and getting along with others. These times present the greatest challenges. It is easy to let days, months, and even years slide past before you realize how many opportunities have been missed to show your children that you value them.

Most people remember to do the right things at times that are out of the ordinary. The difficult task is to remain conscious of your child's or student's need for your acceptance, approval, and love in a demonstrable, tangible way during the routine times. When people show delight because you are part of their life, it is hard not to develop a good feeling about yourself.

You will find additional ideas and examples in *One Hundred Ways to Enhance Self-Concept in the Classroom: A Handbook for Teachers and Parents,* by Jack Canfield and Harold Wells. This book was published in 1976 and may be difficult to find, but it is worth the effort. Also look for *Enhancing Self-Esteem,* by Michele and Craig Borba; this book will be of special interest to elementary teachers, but parents will like it too.

Social Relationships and Social Skills Training

Many children with attention deficit–hyperactivity disorder have difficulty getting along with others. Occasionally, an impulsive child who is well liked at school serves as a model for the rest of the class and achieves high status because of trouble-making behavior, but this is rare. Usually children with ADHD have problems with their peers and are rejected.

Children with ADHD may have difficulty getting along with other children for the same reasons that they have problems with adults. If a child is intrusive, demanding, or unpredictable, other children will be distressed or angered. As children with ADHD get older, their peers may regard them as unreliable and irresponsible just as parents and teachers often do.

Children frequently have difficulty understanding the effect of their behavior on others. As adults, we know how hard it can be to maintain an objective or unemotional view of a child's behavior, so it should not surprise us that other children find it even more of a problem. A child with ADHD may be bewildered by his own behavior and his effect on others.

For some children psychotherapy is helpful, especially therapy that emphasizes group treatment with others the child's age. Individual or family therapy may also prove beneficial. On the other hand, efforts to find some original way to point out to your child the mistakes she makes when she tries to get along with others are usually a waste of time. Lectures explaining how to get along with others are seldom helpful for a child with ADHD.

Many parents and teachers have spent fruitless hours trying to help children understand how their actions have led to unpleasant consequences. At times it seems as if you are getting somewhere and that your child understands what you are saying. Some children do gain insight into the problem. But most often efforts to point out a child's blunders that start on a cooperative note quickly deteriorate into an argument over who was at fault or who started the fight.

Our concern about a child's social skills and social competence arises not only from a desire to help children with ADHD enjoy good social relationships as children, but also because the nature and quality of peer relationships in childhood are related to how well people get along as adults. Social competence affects mental health. In a classic study one research worker found that grade-school peer ratings were more sensitive predictors of later mental health than were any other school records including achievement, IQ, and teachers' judgments.

SOCIAL SKILLS AND SOCIAL COMPETENCE

Social skills are discrete, learned behaviors. Social competence refers to smoothly flowing sequences of many different skills. For example, the ability to greet someone, smile, say hello, and initiate a conversation reflects a sequence of skills. The ability to put these skills together and continue a pleasant social interaction illustrates social competence.

Most of us have adequate social skills. We know how to smile politely when we meet someone, shake hands, and say, "How do you do?" However, there are considerable differences among us in social competence.

There are people you know who, thrust into any situation, conduct themselves with ease and pleasure. Not only do they give every sign of comfort and enjoyment talking to others, but people like to be with them because their sense of social competence is contagious and makes everyone feel comfortable.

There are others who, while they are socially competent, do not have the same social grace. And we have already observed that a child who is socially incompetent is at risk for later psychological difficulties. This probably results from an inability to form positive relationships with peers and authority figures.

When we set out to develop a training program to teach social skills and enhance social competence, we usually divide our task into two segments. First, we must teach some children how to control excesses of behavior. A child may run when he should walk. Another talks when she should be quiet. Our second task is to teach social skills to those who lack them. Controlling excesses of behavior and learning specific skills that are lacking often go hand in hand, but they require different approaches.

If we want to reduce aggression or change bad habits such as talking out of turn or pushing to the front of the line, we often use behavior modification. Medicine is also effective in controlling excessive talking or fighting. But while medication may help control a child who fights or pushes, it will not give a child social skills he does not already possess. These have to be taught.

One of our graduate students studied the peer relationships of children with ADHD by comparing the rankings of the symptoms of ADHD made by children and by teachers. In the first part of the study results confirmed earlier research. There was a high correlation between ratings of peer rejection and many symptoms of ADHD. The relationship was much stronger for boys than for girls.

In the second part of the study 34 children in third and fourth grade were asked to give a rating to each of the 10 items on the Conners' behavior rating scale ranging from "very good behavior" to "very bad behavior." The Conners' rating scales are popular instruments used to assess the presence and severity of symptoms of ADHD. A group of teachers looked at the same 10 items of the Conners' scale and rated each item the same way.

Based on the ratings by children and teachers, the items on the questionnaire were rank-ordered according to how bad the behavior was perceived to be. The items are ranked from 1 to 10 in the order calculated from the children's ratings.

1.	Temper outbursts; explosive, unpredictable behavior	9
2.	Demands must be met immediately; easily frustrated	8
3.	Inattentive; easily distracted	3
4.	Disturbs other children	1
5.	Constantly fighting	2
6.	Restless or overactive	4
7.	Fails to finish things he or she starts	5
8.	Cries often and easily	10
9.	Excitable; impulsive	6
10.	Mood changes quickly	7

The column at the right shows how teachers ranked the seriousness of these behaviors. Most striking is the fact that children and teachers completely disagreed on item 1. In addition, the two items that teachers ranked 1 and 2, "disturbs other children" and "constantly fighting," merited only a middle position on the students' list.

The importance of the comparison does not lie in the details. What is instructive here is the evidence that the behavior that disturbs teachers may not disturb other children. The implication for a social skills training program is that the behaviors and skills we select as targets for treatment must be the ones that are important, not only to adults, but also to children.

If we take time to observe the behavior of children with ADHD as they interact with others, we can learn more that helps us understand why some children have problems getting along with each other. Richard Gelb and Joseph Jacobson, from the Department of Psychology at Wayne State University in Detroit, examined the interaction of popular and unpopular children during cooperative and competitive activities. Although ADHD was not the focus of their study, we know that many children with ADHD are less popular than other children.

Gelb and Jacobson videotaped popular and unpopular fourth-grade boys as each tried to gain entry into a cooperative or competitive task involving classmates who were average in popularity. The researchers noted that during competitive tasks, unpopular children were more likely to break rules, emit silly noises, and appeal to authority.

In the calmer atmosphere of a cooperative project, unpopular children behaved better and the others were more tolerant of them. The authors concluded that the context of the social experience influences the unpopular child's ability to get along.

This helps us understand not only why a child may be unpopular, but also why there is so much variability in behavior and social skills. We have to look closely at children's activities to see that what on the surface may seem to be similar activities are quite different, make different demands on a child, and therefore require dramatically different behavior patterns.

The child with ADHD may play cooperatively at times and at other times may be demanding, aggressive, and angry. This inconsistency often confuses teachers and parents. It makes it seem as if the child's troublesome behavior is willful. We can avoid blaming the child if we understand that behavior may be different in different situations. We can then better determine the nature of our role in offering assistance. Children with ADHD have many problems in social relationships. Russell Barkley, who has done a great deal of research on ADHD, found that 81% of a sample of hyperactive children had problems with their peers compared to only 7% of the normal group. Thomas Achenbach surveyed 1,300 children at mental health clinics and compared them to 1,300 other children, ages 4 to 16. He found that 40% of the difference between the two groups of children was in the categories of poor peer relations and social behavior within the family.

No matter how it is measured, the social standing of children with ADHD is below that of their classmates. Children with ADHD are typically described by their teachers as more troublesome and less welcome in their classroom than children with any other type of disability. We suspect that this finding may reflect not only the difficulty many children with ADHD present in the classroom, but also the relative lack of understanding on the part of teachers about the disorder compared to their knowledge about other commonly occurring school-related problems such as learning disabilities or mental retardation.

Does medication help children in their social relationships? As we have learned over the past few years, different doses of psychostimulants are effective for different symptoms of ADHD. Consequently, we have learned to address the question of whether medication helps children in social situations with more precision. As with so many of the problems children encounter, the effect of medication on social skills becomes more complex as we look into this subject at deeper levels.

For example, if a child takes medication that makes her less impulsive and consequently less unpredictable, other children will probably be happy to play with her. Without the medicine they might reject her. But social competence reflects the accumulation of knowledge, experience, and social skills, so simply making a child less impulsive for several hours may do nothing to improve that child's ability to understand other people or see how her own behavior affects them.

There have been several research studies comparing the social interactions of children with ADHD when taking medication or a placebo. Medication improves scores on tests and rating scales. The most notable effect of medicine is to reduce the controlling behavior of boys with ADHD. They are less bossy and demanding, so they get along better.

Also important is the observation that normal children typically show a reciprocal improvement in their behavior, making them more open to cooperative play and less rejecting and controlling. Although other children may not be able to explain why they are more cooperative with the child who has ADHD, they recognize the change in the child's behavior and this influences their own behavior in return. A child on medication may also be able to take an objective look at his own behavior and understand why he has social problems.

These research findings, backed up by clinical experience, provide some help for the physician and parents who are trying to decide whether to treat a child with ADHD with medication during nonschool hours. We believe that if a child's social relationships are impaired to the point where the child suffers psychologically, then consideration must be given to using medication outside school hours.

We want to highlight one aspect of social relationships where medicine does not appear to be helpful. It does not yield an increase in prosocial behavior. That is, the child with ADHD, even when successfully treated with medication, is not likely to make more positive and constructive overtures to other children. While the decrease in troublesome behavior may encourage others to approach the child with ADHD, parents and teachers must realize that the child with ADHD will require more specific and practical guidance to develop positive social skills. Fortunately, that is easier to accomplish when a child has responded well to medication.

DEVELOPMENT OF SOCIAL COMPETENCE

In order for children to develop social competence, they must have a good self-image. We discussed the development of self-concept in chapter 6, but it should be clear that the child who feels inadequate or who does not trust her own judgment may behave in an awkward manner. She may be influenced to act by how she thinks she should behave or by what other people expect. This denies the child a chance to observe and assess how other people behave as well as denying her the comfort of experimenting with different patterns of behavior herself.

For example, children who feel inadequate are unlikely to smile and offer a greeting if they think that such behavior might cause other people to talk to them. They may fear that they will not know how to respond. Of course, there are many more complex examples, but you can see from this simple illustration that uncertainty about one's self may impair social interactions and the resulting learning experiences at a fundamental level.

Social competence rests on other important building blocks, too. Two important elements are (a) a person's ability to empathize or take the role of the other person and (b) the ability to develop a repertoire of a number of different potential responses to any particular situation.

A person can never know what another person thinks or feels. On the other hand, getting along with other people depends on a reasonable facility in interpreting the overt and subtle clues a person displays that indicate how they feel and what they are thinking about.

Social Imperception

Some children with ADHD suffer from social imperception. Just as children with learning disabilities may have visual or auditory perceptual problems that interfere with their accurate interpretation of what they see or hear, some authorities believe that people with ADHD do not perceive or understand the actions and nonverbal behavior of other people as well as most of us do.

No one is certain why problems with social imperception occur. They may be due to the fact that a person with ADHD is inattentive and consequently misses many small or subtle details, including those needed to understand how people behave. An impulsive person who starts to respond before another person has even completed a sentence is likely to miss elements of body position, facial expression, or even tone of voice that are part of the complete message. So the person with ADHD is likely to respond incorrectly, and his behavior will seem inappropriate or odd to others.

Our ability to understand other people develops over many years and through many different experiences. If in the earliest years a child is denied the opportunity to observe these things, by the time she is older the cumulative effect will be substantial.

When we understand social imperception we realize why efforts to logically discuss an argument or a fight your child was in do not necessarily help the child understand his own role. He may have interpreted the entire set of circumstances differently from you.

We also encounter many children with ADHD who do not know where and how they fit in with friends and classmates. A child may feel that no one likes her although many children do. On the other hand, some children may feel that they are well liked when no one likes them.

A better understanding of imperception also helps us understand why some children find it so difficult to accept responsibility for their own actions. To be sure, there are many reasons why a child may be reluctant to accept blame for trouble, but if a child with ADHD does not know what it is that he did to irritate another child, he may think the other child's angry response is an unprovoked attack. Consequently, after an argument or fight when you ask a child what he did to provoke the other child, he is likely to respond by saying, "I didn't do anything."

We see repeated examples of an impulsive child goading another and teasing long after the other child has insisted that he does not like it. When the other child finally erupts in anger, the child with ADHD expresses pain and surprise and says, "I was only teasing" or "I was only having fun."

If the child with ADHD does not see the other child's anger rising or misinterprets nonverbal communication, he may be telling the truth when he says that he thinks the other child attacked him for no reason.

It is important for parents, teachers, and other professionals to understand why people with ADHD have so many problems. It is not enough to know what the problems are. If we can identify the cause of the difficulty, we will know where to start in order to treat the child. We now know that the most effective approach to treating children with inadequate social skills is group treatment that allows the people with ADHD to understand their weaknesses and then learn to practice the skills that are poorly developed in a safe and supportive small group with others who have similar problems.

Alternative Responses

Getting along well with others does not require that you submerge your own personality, but the ability to understand other people's feelings is necessary for successful social discourse. In addition, being able to "read" other people is a source of valuable information about how you are coming across to them. Based on their responses, you can modify your own behavior to give the impression you intend.

As we speak or work with others, each of us usually has a choice of a number of different ways in which to talk or behave. Our voices may be loud or soft, our gaze intense or gentle, our gestures casual or flamboyant. The words we choose, the way we hold our bodies, and our tone of voice all are part of our communication. For most of our routine day-to-day activities we do not give these choices a great deal of thought, but even in the simplest circumstances, we have choices. In more complex situations, we may have to choose from a number of different ways to act and speak or to avoid acting and speaking.

The ability to pause and recognize the alternative responses available is especially important at times of interpersonal conflict. For example, if you are upset with your spouse, how you express your displeasure may be very important. Possible responses even include not responding at all and letting the matter pass. However, if you are particularly frustrated, you may confront the issue directly in a harsh tone, in a gentle supportive manner, or by treating it as a joke. You may be overtly critical of your spouse or you may take the responsibility yourself or phrase your complaint in terms of your discomfort or dissatisfaction rather than by outright criticism.

When conflict arises, a high degree of social competence allows a person to select the behavior that is most likely to achieve his goal. For example, if someone insults you and hurts your feelings, you may become angry and respond harshly in order to hit back at the person who hurt you. But there are other responses you could choose. If your goal is to alert the other person to the fact that you were hurt and to discourage him from harming you in the future, you would not want to lash out in an effort to cause him pain. Instead, you would probably say that the remark hurt you and that you would appreciate it if he would not talk to you in that way in the future.

Of course, you have a huge number of response choices, and there is no single best way to respond. Usually, the more choices people can generate, the more likely it is that they will choose one that will accomplish their goal without causing any additional discomfort, embarrassment, or distress.

Someone who has ADHD is at a disadvantage because of the tendency to behave impulsively. Acting quickly, often without thinking at all, eliminates the opportunity to consider the many different ways of responding. Nevertheless, it is terribly frustrating when an adult continually asks a child, "Why don't you think before you speak?" or "Why didn't you stop to think before you did that?"

Questions that ask a person with ADHD to explain her behavior or account for why she did or did not do something are doomed to failure. What do you expect your 10-year-old to do when you ask her why she lashed out angrily at a classmate who made a face at her and got in trouble with the principal? Would you be satisfied if she sat down and explained that she had ADHD and reminded you that self-control is difficult for her? The response most parents and teachers would make to an answer like this is "You can't use that as an excuse. You are responsible for your own behavior."

One of the most frustrating experiences for a child with ADHD is to respond honestly to questions only to find that others will not accept the answer. Even when a child tries to explain his own behavior, his explanations are usually not satisfying to his questioners. Finally, the child learns to shrug his shoulders and give up trying to explain.

There are circumstances, of course, when any of us may behave impulsively or in a way that we later regret. We have all had the experience of stopping after a heated moment and considering what we have said or done, then coming up with very much better ways of responding and wishing we could play the scene over again. These experiences, how ever, occur infrequently. For the person with ADHD, they are frequent occurrences in both simple and complex situations. As a consequence, the person with ADHD accumulates the burden of many clumsy and inappropriate responses in interactions with other people. This not only makes the person feel inadequate and is an assault to her self-esteem, but it also undermines her confidence in her ability to deal effectively with social situations in the future. For some people, this may lead to an avoidance of social relationships. For others, these experiences may increase anxiety and cause them to be even more impulsive and, consequently, even more vulnerable to clumsy and inappropriate behavior.

Psychologist Steven Landau and his colleagues at Illinois State University have studied the social communication patterns of boys with ADHD. In one intriguing project they used a television talk show format. Seventeen boys with ADHD who were in the third through sixth grades were paired with normal children from the same school. Landau and his associates were careful to exclude children with learning disabilities.

In the TV talk show game, one child played the role of the host of the show and the other played his guest. Each child took turns playing both roles. The scenes were videotaped and carefully analyzed.

Analysis revealed that boys with ADHD had more communication problems. For example, they were less able to adjust the way they spoke and behaved according to the demands of a particular situation. Being the host or the guest required a child to behave in different ways. Children who did not have ADHD were able to fit the patterns of their verbal behavior to the role they were playing. Children with ADHD were less likely to be able to make this adjustment.

Another interesting finding from this study was that while the behavior of the boys with ADHD did not change in response to a change in either their role or their partner's behavior, the behavior of the normal partners did alter in order to maintain equilibrium with the child with ADHD. That is, although the child with ADHD might not have been able to read the other child or the demands of the circumstances properly and adjust his behavior accordingly, the other child usually made some effort to accommodate the child with ADHD.

Many people who live with a person with ADHD find that they must make many adjustments in order to maintain balance and peace in the home. There are literally thousands of small adjustments to routines and life experiences necessary to maintain harmony. Even younger brothers and sisters do this, often without awareness.

At some point, even the most caring people become frustrated, however, and they may decide that enough is enough; they are no longer going to go out of their way to continue to make adjustments for the other person. This serves as further evidence for the person with ADHD that his life is filled with seemingly arbitrary events, many of which are negative and hurtful, that occur through no fault or action of his own.

We believe that teaching children to be socially competent is not emphasized enough in public education. This is especially true in the case of children with learning or behavioral problems. Along with an abundance of research studies, common sense has led us to the conclusion that children who have emotional problems, learning difficulties, or other handicaps are especially dependent on their ability to get along with other people and move about comfortably in society. Learning social skills in order to become a socially competent adult takes on critical importance in the lives of many children with ADHD.

Examples do not have to be dramatic to illustrate the burden a lack of social competence causes. Paul was 16 years old. He had ADHD and a mild learning disability. His school career had been difficult. Shortly after Paul's 16th birthday, he began to express his impatience with his parents' reluctance to allow him to get a driver's license. They explained that they were concerned about his ability to control his behavior and they wanted to defer his license for 6 months, until they had a chance to watch him drive and he had a chance to become somewhat more mature.

Both of Paul's parents agreed that if Paul had a job, they would let him drive to and from work, and that success on the job would be one way in which he could demonstrate the maturity and responsibility his parents thought necessary in order to grant him greater driving privileges.

As time went on and Paul failed to get a job, his parents became increasingly irritated. They grew angry seeing Paul waste time; they thought that, since he was old enough to work, he ought to have some sort of part-time job just to keep busy. They told him that they would no longer give him spending money, although they would continue to provide for all of his other needs.

Paul became enraged. He criticized his parents for their neglect, insisting that they did not care about him. He said that he did not know why he stayed in their home, since they were not fulfilling even minimal parental responsibilities.

Paul's parents were astonished. They had no idea what caused his outburst. When they were able to respond, they did so in an argumentative fashion and tried to explain to Paul that he was old enough to have a job and that they thought it was a good way for him to demonstrate his responsibility. The argument deteriorated further, and they used his outburst as an illustration of his irresponsibility and lack of maturity and as a further reason to deny him a driver's license.

A parent who has raised a child with ADHD knows that arguments of this kind go nowhere. They only add to the pain and widen the gulf between parents and teenagers.

Another event that helps us to understand Paul better occurred one day when the family was on its way to an appointment in our office. Although at first glance, this occurrence does not seem connected to Paul's failure to get a job, the two events are intimately associated. Before coming to our office Paul had an earlier appointment with his family doctor to review his treatment with medication. The physician's office was always crowded and patients were admitted on a first-come, first-served basis, so when patients arrived they put their name on a sign-up sheet at the receptionist's desk.

Parking was difficult in the area, and Paul's mother stopped in front of the doctor's office building and suggested that Paul go into the office, put his name on the sign-up sheet, and wait for her. She told him that she would be in as soon as she parked.

Suddenly Paul, who had been quite pleasant until then, became angry. He told his mother that he thought it was a foolish idea. He began to complain about how long they had to wait in the doctor's office and ended his tirade by saying that he was sick and tired of taking his medicine because it was not helping him anyway.

Paul's mother did not know what was happening. She fastened on the first sensible argument she could think of in order to make Paul calm down. She explained that he had taken medicine for several years, that it helped him, and that he had to continue. At least, she insisted, he should go into the office and explain to the doctor how he felt.

Paul and his mother continued to argue about the value of the medicine. They finally parked the car, but when they reached the doctor's office they were both very angry. The appointment with Paul's physician was routine. Paul did not discuss his concern about the medicine, he accepted the new prescription, and the matter seemed to be behind him. Several hours later they arrived for Paul's appointment in our office, and one of us had a chance to review what had happened and then go over the experience with Paul and his mother.

After several months of psychotherapy, Paul had gained enough insight to be able to explain to his mother and therapist the feelings that had given rise to his behavior. He explained that he was embarrassed to go into the doctor's office and put his name on the list. He feared that his mother would be impatient if he tried to explain his embarrassment because he did not fully understand, himself, why he felt awkward walking into the physician's office and crossing the room to the registration desk.

As we talked, he expressed some of his concerns. He felt that people were watching him as he walked across the room and that made him uncomfortable. He worried that the sign-up sheet might not be on the counter and he did not know how to ask for it. He was afraid that he might make a mistake and was concerned that the receptionist might ask him a question he could not answer.

Two sets of problems crippled Paul. First, he was embarrassed by his inadequacies in a very simple social situation. Second, his mother was unaware of the extent of his feelings of inadequacy. Even if she had understood them, she would probably have dismissed Paul's concerns, saying something like "Paul, you're 16 years old. Just go in there and put your name on the list."

These barriers to effective communication backed Paul into a corner where he was flooded with anxiety and where desperation clouded his judgment. He seized the first excuse he could think of to avoid going into the doctor's office alone.

Fortunately, Paul's mother listened carefully and responded with her heart as well as her head. This, in turn, allowed the therapist to turn the discussion to Paul's failure to get a job and Paul was able to explain to his mother that his reluctance to seek a job reflected much of this same social discomfort; he did not know how to walk into a store or business and say that he was looking for work.

As Paul's case illustrates, many people lack social skills and confidence at such a fundamental level that other members of their family as well as their teachers, friends, and associates find their behavior hard to understand. Many social problems, if left untreated, can have a harmful effect on a person's ability to get along with others, but if they are recognized early they can usually be treated with hope for considerable improvement.

HELPING CHILDREN GAIN SOCIAL COMPETENCE

Traditional Psychotherapy

There are many ways to try to help children develop social skills, but the development of social competence may not come quickly for the child with ADHD. The most successful treatment programs emphasize a high degree of structure in a group setting. The counselor or therapist usually takes a very active role by providing specific goals for each treatment session and a carefully focused plan that defines how each child will participate.

Traditional forms of psychotherapy provide little benefit for children with ADHD who have serious social problems. Although many people have problems getting along with others because of deep-seated psychological conflicts within themselves, the social problems of most children with ADHD do not represent mental problems, but are the consequences of the symptoms of the disorder. Lack of social competence is not strictly speaking a psychological disorder or a symptom of a mental problem.

Many parents, teachers, and psychotherapists have had lengthy discussions with children with ADHD to help them gain a more objective point of view about social problems. For example, a child may insist that he is never at fault when there is a fight on the playground or a girl may be unaware of her intrusive, controlling behavior with the other girls that causes them to reject her, leaving her sadder, but no wiser, about her social feelings.

You can spend a lot of time discussing how to avoid conflict or make friends, but even though a child may gain some understanding and a broader perspective on these events, there is usually little behavioral change. After all, if a child perceives the situation differently from others it does no good to stress his responsibility. He responds on the basis of his interpretation of events.

Lectures or advice are equally ineffective. You may explain how to approach other children at play in order to be invited to join in or you may provide instructions on how to engage in social chit-chat; you may even coach children about what to say.

Children usually agree and promise to follow these suggestions next time. "Next time" rarely comes because when another occasion arises, anxiety or self-doubt cripple even the best intentions and plans.

Social skills deficits are frequently accompanied by social anxiety. Children as well as adults are overly concerned about what other people are thinking about them. They fear that they will say something foolish or act in a way that will make others think badly of them. Even in the absence of rejection or criticism, the socially inadequate person often spends a great deal of time going over what was said (and not said) with a critical eye. Sometimes this critical review convinces a person that she behaved badly and that the other people are confirmed in their negative opinion about her.

Social anxiety cannot be treated only with psychological interpretations and advice about how to act next time. In addition, since the ability of many people with ADHD to appraise social circumstances is faulty, they cannot adjust their own behavior properly in response to other people's reactions to them.

Children as Therapists

We have been favorably impressed by several programs that have used popular children to help less popular or socially isolated children in the classroom. These programs are helpful with rejected children as well as neglected or isolated children. The plans follow common sense. Popular children are given instructions and guidance, which sensitizes them to the feelings of the less popular child.

The treatment program has two parts. There is a series of organized sessions, but the day-to-day activities of the children provide the best milieu in which to effect any change. For example, the popular children are asked to greet less popular children every day and to praise and compliment them when they deserve it. Initiating conversation with less popular children boosts their self-esteem. The popular child is also a model for other children in school who become more willing to make overtures to the less popular child.

The popular children also serve as models for the socially isolated child. They are encouraged to share themselves, which breaks down some of the barriers between isolated children and others. Many of the experiences that occur spontaneously are then rehearsed and become the subject for role playing.

There are drawbacks as well as advantages to programs that utilize other children as participants. The chief advantage lies in the fact that programs that call on the resources of other children are not confined to an hour or two a week or to a special room or office. Classmates are present 25 to 35 hours a week, and the growth of the child with ADHD takes place as part of ordinary activities, not in the artificial environment of a treatment room.

The disadvantage of these programs lies in the need to invest a great deal of care to ensure that the children who are therapists do not feel stressed or become so caught up in their own status that they develop a controlling relationship with the child with ADHD.

Helena Middleton and her co-workers developed an interesting program in four schools in Davis County, Utah. Middleton identified 96 children with social skills problems and assigned them randomly to either experimental or comparison groups. Students in the experimental group were assigned a student peer facilitator (SPF).

Middleton and others met once a week with the SPFs for about 20 minutes. The children were instructed in intervention techniques and assignments were made to work with one or more of the children in the experimental group. The assignments were done on a rotating basis so the SPFs worked with a number of different children. School principals, teachers, and parents were invited to the sessions in order to observe and offer suggestions.

In the early stages the SPFs were asked to greet every child in a positive way each day, praise or compliment the child in social and academic areas, and identify inappropriate behaviors that would be targets for later intervention. As the weeks went on, the SPFs were asked to become more involved in the target child's life and by the fifth and sixth sessions they were providing guidance and suggestions for the children with problems. During all of this time the facilitators were asked to be as supportive as possible, to offer help when appropriate, and to maintain contact by telephone if the child was not involved in regular activities or was absent from school.

The results of the project were gratifying. Boys and girls who had social skills problems were accepted more by other children following treatment. When compared to the social acceptance of the children who had been in the control group and never received special treatment, there were striking differences.

The program lasted only 2 months, so we do not know what the long-term effects are. Some children with social skills problems may have continued to do well, but it is reasonable to expect that some would drift back to their earlier habits once the support was withdrawn. This still needs to be studied, although we know from other research that most social skills training programs usually must be maintained for a long time, often for years.

Notice the high degree of structure and organization of the therapy program in Davis County. Treatment was successful because the activities of the student therapists were specific and carefully adhered to. Michael Sancilio of the Department of Psychology at the University of Minnesota surveyed similar research and concluded that just increasing a child's contact with peers does not do much good. The interaction has to be structured and have specific goals in order to be an effective technique. Children with deficient social skills need to be taught the social skills that they lack in a very clear, explicit, and highly organized way.

Structured Learning

Structured learning is a teaching and therapeutic approach designed to provide children with instruction in the development of social skills. Perhaps it ought to be called *very* structured learning. Emphasis is placed on the development of a clear-cut series of exercises and activities. The primary elements of structured learning include (a) modeling, (b) role playing, (c) performance feedback, and (d) transfer of training.

A full discussion of structured learning is beyond the scope of this book, but we want to give you enough information so that you can decide whether to establish a structured social skills program for your children.

In structured learning each skill to be taught is broken down into small constituent parts or steps. Students are shown examples of people performing each part (modeling). The children then practice the skill (role playing) and get feedback on their performance. Participants are given homework assignments that encourage them to practice the new skill so that it will be transferred to other settings. These four components are at the core of any social skills training program.

For many children it is necessary to begin with very basic social skills. For example, many children do not know how to greet someone. Even before we address social anxiety, we have to be certain that the child has the skills to greet another child, even if it is only to say hello. If you know how to do it, saying hello may not seem like an important skill, but if you lack the skill, it is an immense problem. A related but more complex skill is learning how to approach a small group of children who are already engaged in conversation or an activity and ask to join them.

Other examples of basic social skills that are taught include:

Introducing yourself

Giving positive feedback

Receiving positive feedback

Offering to help

Asking for clear instructions

Sending an "I'm interested" message

Sending an ignoring message

Learning how to join a conversation

These lessons not only build up a repertoire of skills, but also help children to develop self-confidence. In addition, these early experiences in the structured learning group let the child see that social skills can be learned and introduce the child to the procedures of the group. Subsequently, when more complex social problems are introduced, such as handling name calling and teasing or learning to say no to stay out of trouble, the child has sufficient experience to continue to benefit from the program.

It is not difficult to teach most children social skills of the type discussed here. It is, however, very difficult to ensure that the skills are transferred outside of the classroom or treatment room into other areas of the child's life. Homework assignments are one of the main ways to encourage this transfer of training. In essence, children are instructed to try out what they have learned in real life.

Homework assignments begin with the teacher and student together deciding when and how the child will use the skill; they progress to the point where students make these decisions and monitor their own behavior. In the early stages the evaluation of the child's performance is focused on how well the child implements the skills rather than whether the child is successful in social interaction.

In chapter 8, Dr. Stephen Hillman explains how to teach children to be less impulsive and gain better understanding of themselves in order to control their behavior and improve relationships with other people. If you are interested in starting a social skills training program in your school or community, you will find the following references helpful:

1. *Skill Streaming the Elementary Child: A Guide for Teaching Prosocial Skills*, by Ellen McGinnis, Arnold Goldstein, Arnold Sprafkin, and Nancy Gershaw. This book, published in 1984, can be obtained from Research Press in Champaign, Illinois.

2. *Getting Along with Others: Teaching Social Effectiveness to Children*, by Nance Jackson, Donald Jackson, and Kathy Monroe. This 1983 book is also available from Research Press, Champaign, Illinois.

3. *Social Solutions Curriculum*, by Robert Weisberger. Published in 1983, this can be ordered from the American Institute for Research, Palo Alto, California.

8

Cognitive Behavior Therapy
Stephen Hillman, PhD*

Cognitive behavior therapy (CBT) refers to techniques used to change children's behavior that focus on how children think. Psychologists use the term *cognitive* to refer to thinking. CBT is based on the assumption that behavior is a consequence of how people interpret their experiences, not the result of the events themselves. Our previous discussion of the development of self-esteem placed a similar emphasis on what an experience means to an individual.

Cognitive behavior therapists make several additional assumptions about thinking and behavior. How we think naturally affects how we behave. Our behavior, in turn, has an effect on the behavior of others. The cycle continues, as the behavior of others affects us in turn. So, according to behavior therapists, we create our own social environment.

An aggressive boy may expect other children to treat him in a hostile way. This expectation causes the child to act aggressively ("I'll get them

*Dr. Hillman is on the faculty of Wayne State University, Detroit, Michigan, where he is the head of the Department of Educational Psychology.

before they get me"), thus provoking aggression from others and strengthening the initial expectations of the child. Expecting trouble creates a hostile environment and trouble often follows.

Another child, facing a difficult homework assignment, puts it off because she believes she cannot be successful. Avoiding homework will probably result in a poor grade, thus reinforcing the child's perception that she cannot do the work.

By emphasizing changes in how people think, CBT is a valuable addition to a list of therapies that includes medication, behavior modification, curriculum changes, and family counseling.

As children mature their thinking changes. In the early years, a lot of thinking is controlled by parents, then teachers, and only later by the children themselves as they move toward greater independence. During preschool years, parents take much of the responsibility for solving problems. During this time, parents usually talk about the cognitive strategies they use in problem solving and hope their children will learn by example.

For instance, a parent assembling a toy car from printed instructions might say aloud, "First I have to find all the parts and then hold the frame next to the picture to see which end is the front and where the seat goes."

In this way the child sees how a parent works and also learns the thinking process behind the actions. In other cases the parent might give advice on how to greet a friend, lose a game, resolve a dispute over a toy, or negotiate a favorable bedtime. As children get older, they assume more responsibility and, eventually, we expect adolescents to make correct decisions and solve problems in their day-to-day activities themselves.

As children become more mature, parents and teachers move from direct modifications of the child's behavior to discussion, reason, negotiation, and joint decision making. You may tell your 4-year-old daughter, "Let Katy have a turn dressing the doll, now," but you would probably tell your 8-year-old, "I would like the two of you to figure out a way to share your toy." If they still need help you can intervene, preferably as a mediator, guiding the girls to a successful resolution of their problem rather than imposing a solution of your own.

As children acquire new skills, we try to ensure that these skills will be used in many different situations. Each new set of circumstances presents special challenges as well as opportunities, and skills may not be easily transferred from one situation to another. Modification of a child's knowledge and thinking patterns along with changes in the child's habits should yield better self-control.

PROBLEM-SOLVING TECHNIQUES

Teaching problem-solving techniques utilizes a number of components. These include (a) response-delay training, (b) self-instruction, (c) reinforcement, (d) modeling or demonstrations by an adult, (e) role playing, and (f) training in feelings identification.

Response-Delay Training

Response-delay training teaches children to stop and think before they act. We help children learn strategies to slow down and think by increasing the amount of time before they say or do something.

Response-delay training requires an adult to teach a child to repeat self-directing phrases at crucial times. "I must slow down" and "I must think before acting" are examples of self-directing phrases.

Our goal is to help children recognize when response-delay techniques are needed and do them on their own, but at first, these verbal commands are taught through direct instruction and modeling.

For example, one parent taught her 9-year-old son to stop, put his hand on the knob of the kitchen door before leaving for school, and say to himself, "Stop. Think. Read."

Posted on the door was a list of things he would need for school. At the top of the list was the question, "Have I remembered to take . . . ?" This was followed by a list that included "book," "book bag," "lunch," "my coat," "my hat," and several other items.

Think about how much attention to detail a plan like this requires. Everything is simple and straightforward, but it is also carefully thought out. By placing his hand on the doorknob the child is forced to come to a complete stop. In the early stages of training, the boy's mother stood at the door, her hand holding his, clutching the knob, as she read the list to him. She let him see how she carefully reviewed all the items and performed each necessary step before opening the door and letting him set off for school.

Most parents would prefer that their children do a mental rehearsal of this sort while getting dressed, brushing their teeth, or eating breakfast. In fact, that is how most people operate. A child with ADHD needs more structure and careful instructions in a step-by-step process to learn response-delay techniques.

Unfortunately, in many cases, these techniques are introduced at the wrong time—for example, after a child has just done something impulsively. The parent shouts, "Why don't you think before you act?" or "Count to ten before you hit your sister." These comments attempt to modify the thoughts and behaviors of the child to produce better response-delay actions, but they are implemented in the wrong way at the wrong time. Response-delay training is most effective when it is done calmly. Explain what you would like your child to do. Act it out. Voice the thoughts you have and the things you tell yourself so your child can learn what to do. Then, playing the part of your child or student, go through the thoughts and actions step by step. This is called *role playing*.

Self-Instruction

Once the child has restrained herself from impulsive action, she is ready to organize a strategy to deal with her problem. Self-instruction refers to self-control statements that keep children on the problem-solving track. The statements are cues that organize the problem-solving effort. A self-statement such as, "Let's see, what am I supposed to do?" helps a child slow down before taking action, ask questions about what has to be done, and think about the needed steps.

Self-control statements fall into five categories:

1. Identification of the problem. ("Okay, this is a math problem. I have to multiply and then add.")

2. Specification of the specific strategies to use. ("I'll start with the 1's column and borrow from the 10's column.")

3. Attention-focusing statements. ("I will take one step at a time. First, do I have to borrow?")

4. Self-rewarding statements. ("Good, that's done right. Now do the 10's column.")

5. Statements that help the child cope with failure and reduce the amount of time spent complaining or criticizing. In the face of failure or an inability to solve a problem, many children say to themselves, "I must really be stupid," or "I guess I can't do anything right." We must arm children with more constructive self-instructions. For example, "This isn't going right. I think I will stop and start over from the beginning," or "I'll try one more time and then I will ask Mom for help."

Reinforcement

Reinforcement includes praise or tokens. It is often a good idea in the early stages, when we are teaching children to modify their thinking patterns with self-instruction and response-delay techniques, to set up a program of behavior modification using rewards for persistence at the task and cooperation. A child who can earn tokens or points to be turned in for special privileges has an added incentive. Do anything you can do to encourage the child to participate in this activity.

Modeling

CBT programs rely heavily on modeling. Parents, therapists, and teachers demonstrate the problem-solving process. Self-control statements are spoken out loud. An adult demonstrates the best way to approach a task or problem. This includes consideration of different approaches to the problem.

Adults and children take turns solving problems, providing parents and teachers with opportunities for further demonstrations and feedback. The child also has an opportunity to practice the new skills.

After a child has learned some self-control techniques, it is helpful for an adult to demonstrate how to cope with mistakes and frustration. Parents can demonstrate the use of appropriate coping self-statements such as "I see I made a mistake. Oh well, if I try again maybe I can get it right." Do not lecture. Give only a little advice. Demonstrate. Model. Act it out.

Teach children how to deal with frustration and anger when their efforts are unsuccessful. People who are successful at solving problems learn to say, "Darn, I'm mad. I'd better stop for a minute and calm down if I want to get this done."

A parent might say aloud, so his son can hear, "My boss gave me more work today and I had other things planned. I was so angry with him I just wanted to scream, or quit my job. Instead I said to myself, calm down. It's really not that bad. You're just frustrated. Relax for a while and then get back to work."

Modeling self-control demonstrates how to think through different situations. Children see how this method of thinking can be used to develop self-control. Modeling and demonstration will not change the behavior of your children immediately, but over time, it will be effective.

These are not lessons you can teach in a few brief sessions. Formal instruction must go on for weeks and even months. You must integrate these procedures into your child's daily routines so they get booster shots and continuing lessons in how cognitive behavior modification works. You are the best model children have. The more they observe how you accomplish practical solutions to problems, the better they will be able to accomplish this themselves.

Role Playing

Newly acquired problem-solving skills should be practiced through role playing. Establish a scenario in which a child can practice the application of self-control skills. Role playing provides an opportunity for practice and feedback and promotes generalization of the new techniques to a wide range of experiences.

During role playing, an adult often takes the role of a child to act out the proper problem-solving behavior and, of course, to speak aloud the accompanying thoughts.

Children and adults also may take the roles of other people in cooperative enterprises or conflicts. This gives a child an opportunity to talk to himself, view the situation from a different perspective, and try out different ways of solving the problem.

Feelings Identification Training

This training teaches children to recognize and describe their own emotions as well as the feelings of others. Children are taught to interpret facial expressions and other body language and to understand the effects of experiences on feelings and the effect of self-statements on their own emotions. First as models, then as coaches, adults guide children through the use and mastery of these techniques.

We begin to teach children to recognize and deal with emotions by making the need for recognizing emotions clear. Explain why it is important to recognize when a playmate or adult is happy, angry, or sad.

Show pictures of facial expressions that characterize the emotion. Have your child practice naming the emotions evident in the faces and the expressions of characters in books, newspaper photographs, pictures from the family album, and even children's comic books and cartoons. Label the emotions. Help the child learn that we have words to describe the feelings we see in other people's actions and facial characteristics.

Then give some personal examples. Ask the child to role play feelings and express them clearly. Use a mirror. Move to the next step. Use pictures and again have the child identify the emotions expressed in people's expressions. Ask what might have provoked the emotion. Talk about the feelings. Make up stories. Use different pictures and repeat the lessons.

These steps can be used to teach children about many emotions: anxiety, pride, disappointment, jealousy, confidence, embarrassment, and others. If you have a video recorder you can make videotapes of the child's emotional reactions and play them back followed by a discussion of the child's thoughts and feelings.

APPLYING PROBLEM SOLVING TO ACADEMIC TASKS

We can train children to use more effective, less impulsive strategies to do schoolwork. Follow these steps:

1. An adult works on a math, science, or language arts exercise while describing to herself aloud what she is doing.

2. The child performs the same task under the direction of the adult, who provides gentle suggestions and corrections.

3. The child performs the task by herself without guidance, while instructing herself out loud.

4. The child keeps practicing, whispering the instructions to herself as she proceeds.

5. Finally, the child learns to silently guide herself with self-instruction. Self-control is our goal.

You must allow the child to see and hear how you take each step. Do not skip any steps or any of your own thoughts. When we face a task or problem, our first efforts have to be directed toward problem identification. We ask ourselves, "Okay, what is being asked of me?" We then focus our own attention by saying to ourselves, "Okay, I understand now. I'll begin to do it." Next, we reinforce ourselves: "I'm doing fine. This is the way to do it. Nice job."

As we move along, we all deal with mistakes. We correct our errors and explain them to ourselves: "Oh no, I made a mistake; well I can go back and fix it, no big deal."

Make sure your child or student hears you think about each of these steps. Use a variety of training tasks. If you want to help with schoolwork, start with simple jobs such as copying squares or triangles or coloring. Move on to simple math problems, then more complex math, understanding short stories, or organizing or writing a paragraph or essay.

Variety is important to maintain motivation. The tasks must also fit the child's age. Remember that children proceed at their own pace; the amount of time needed will vary from child to child.

Demonstrations by adults are not enough to change children's habits or work style. The children must rehearse the skills and be encouraged to try. Use reinforcement to maintain attention and motivation during training.

With all this advice, it may still be hard to involve children in a treatment program. Do not be stuffy. Let your enthusiasm show. You will create higher levels of motivation than with more formal approaches.

Lessons should begin with interesting games, not schoolwork. Games provide an opportunity to teach strategies where there is no history of failure. Do not rush through the early stages of training to get on to "real problems."

When you are demonstrating self-instruction to children, be careful not to use stiff, memorized self-instructions. If we expect children to use the cognitive strategies we teach, we must use words they would use. Ask the following question: "If this child were to think about this problem in a more reflective manner, what words would he use?"

INTERPERSONAL PROBLEM-SOLVING AND SOCIAL SKILLS TRAINING

We used to hope that children with self-control problems who received training in academic problem solving would automatically transfer their new skills to social settings. That was wishful thinking. Additional skills and more training are necessary if we hope to help children with ADHD get along better with their peers. We discussed the importance of social skills training in chapter 7. Interpersonal cognitive problem-solving skills must also be taught, just as we must teach math skills or help a child learn how to complete an assignment.

Many children do not recognize problems when they arise in everyday social situations. This may reflect social imperception and result in misinterpretation of their experience. Sometimes a simple lack of attention to their surroundings causes children to fail to recognize the early stages of escalating conflict. Our early efforts must be directed toward helping a child recognize the cues that indicate something wrong in his relationship with one or a group of children. It is not realistic to expect a child to have problem-solving ideas if he has not first recognized that a problem exists.

Model alternative thinking. That is, demonstrate that there are many solutions to most problems and that it is important to consider more than one before deciding on a course of action. For example, if you are teased, you can tease back, but you can also ignore the problem, explain your hurt feelings, walk away, tell an adult, or punch your tormentor in the nose.

Many examples of cognitive behavior training can be applied to a single child, but training children to develop better interpersonal problem-solving skills usually works best in a group.

After a child has learned to recognize problems in everyday social situations, she is ready to learn how to cope with the problems more effectively. Children in a group should be about the same age. Determine what sorts of problems they are having. This will highlight specific skill deficits. Take care to also identify well-developed social skills; they are strengths to build on.

Many children with social problems have common difficulties. For example, peer group entry is a problem for many children. They do not know how to become part of a group or how to cope with being excluded from it. Another typical social skills problem is the child's response to provocation. How does he deal with teasing? How does he feel and react when he is picked on? A third common trouble spot is the difficulty children with ADHD have dealing with failure. This includes failure at academic tasks, failure to reach established goals, and failure in relationships.

Social skills training begins only after some progress has been made in the area of academic problem solving if these skills have also been deficient. The reason for this is twofold. The child will have had some experience with the techniques of cognitive behavior management and will also have developed self-confidence in applying them.

Since it is hard for some children to take responsibility for their own behavior, begin with problems for which they will accept responsibility.

Both children and adults must know the goals of treatment. When children attempt to solve social problems incorrectly, their child's incorrect solutions must be distinguished from the original problem. For example, if a child hits someone for teasing her, hitting is the child's solution, not the problem. Helping the child find a better response to teasing is the problem. It is not always easy to define the problem, but you will make no progress until you do.

Once the target problem has been selected, take extra time to clarify goals. Do not accept just any goal. Guide the child in selecting a useful goal that can be applied to behaviors to solve his problem. This may be difficult because of the child's low level of awareness and unwillingness to accept responsibility.

If, for example, our goal is to help the child find a better response to another child's teasing, he must be helped to understand that regardless of

146 Management of Children and Adolescents with Attention Deficit–Hyperactivity Disorder

who has responsibility for the initial provocation, he must accept the responsibility for a constructive solution.

The same steps used to control impulsivity and more effectively complete schoolwork are also applicable in social situations. The child can be taught to stop and identify the problem, generate alternative solutions, and select a measured response in a thoughtful way.

Whether we are addressing problems or impulse control, schoolwork or interpersonal relationships, one clear guideline emerges from research and clinical experience. CBT can be helpful in many cases, but it is rare if a child's thoughts and behavior patterns are permanently altered to such an extent that she no longer has difficulties. The most effective CBT programs provide continuing support, group meetings, rehearsal, and review.

A program's failure can often be traced to its brevity. Programs also fail because we do not realize that once formal supervision and instruction are concluded, the behavior patterns of ADHD will return to dominate the child's behavior unless substantial effort is made to help the child continue to apply the lessons learned from CBT.

9

Management of
Selected Behavioral Problems

In this chapter we will review the management of behavioral problems that commonly occur in families with difficult or strong-willed children. Getting up and dressing, mealtime, and bedtime can be particularly stressful. Other problems include the struggle over room maintenance and, as children get older, deciding how much freedom they should have, weighing adolescent demands for autonomy against their need for supervision. Few parents of children with ADHD have escaped the frustration of trying to control their child in public. Finally, we will discuss ways to reduce aggressive behavior.

STARTING THE DAY

Children must get up and get dressed every morning, yet in many homes this routine turns into guerilla warfare. Parents and children usually have tight schedules in the morning, so there is a ready battleground on which to fight for control. Passive aggressive behavior emerges. For the defiant child this may be an opportunity to exert some control over the family.

Most adults like to awake pleasantly. Children are no different. We hear parents describe how they wake their child and then become increasingly frustrated with each return to the child's room to persuade him to get out of bed or to get dressed. This often leads to shouts of anger, threats, and tears until finally parents and children leave the house angry with each other. "She gets everybody's day off to a bad start," one father said.

Many children use parents like snooze alarms. The parents wake the child who, at first, has no intention of getting up because he knows his parents will return in a few minutes with a second call. Snooze alarms do not experience frustration, but parents do as they realize that they will be late for work or their child will be late for school.

We recommend that parents cheerfully wake their child in the morning and then say that they will not be back again. If children do not get up in time they should experience the natural consequence of being late for school. Teachers will usually inquire where they have been or impose a mild punishment. Most children do not like attention paid to them—even entering the class late creates a healthy feeling of embarrassment. Being late for school a few times is not going to hurt a child, but it can be a powerful incentive for the child to better organize himself in the morning.

Parents may have to arrange to be late to work for a few days, but it is unusual for a child to go school late more than twice. Sit quietly near the door and tell your child to let you know when she is ready. You will be pleased to see your child scramble to get out the door on time when it becomes her responsibility and you no longer need to nag. It is hard not to smile when you hear your child urging you to move faster so that she will not be late for school.

GETTING DRESSED

When children and parents become locked into a battle over getting dressed, control or dependency are usually underlying issues. Parents often will not allow their child to dress as he likes. The child who goes to school with mismatched socks, poorly matched shirt and pants, or holes in the knees of jeans may make parents feel that others will judge them negatively. Children sense their parents' sensitivity and manipulate them.

We have found that when dressing becomes a problem it is best for parents either to allow their children to dress as they please or to suggest one or two outfits and then leave it up to them to make the final choice. We often hear parents report that their children ask them what to wear; when a suggestion is made the children reject it. Parents then get frustrated and angry and try to exert even more control, which further inflames the situation. If you make a suggestion and it is rejected, withdraw from the conflict and force your child to make the decision alone. This will immediately end the power struggle.

Battles for control must be distinguished from the need your child might have for supervision while she dresses. Some children with ADHD are so distractible and disorganized that they need someone nearby to provide structure and support. In this case, provide minimal, but needed, supervision.

Overly dependent children also turn to their parents to make decisions they could make themselves. Remember, dependency is a two-way street. Both parties in an overdependent relationship must participate or the overdependency will end. Dependency is like a tug of war. If one party lays down the rope, the struggle stops.

Most adults become better problem solvers with each passing year. This is because they have had the opportunity to solve many problems and learn from doing so. They even learn from mistakes. Children also need to practice solving problems to experience success and failure. A jury of the children's peers stands ready to help. Children must dress according to the standards of their peer group or they will be criticized. If a child dresses in a way that is acceptable to his classmates, he is dressing within normal limits even if his parents disapprove of a temporary style or fad.

MEALTIME

Mealtime is a difficult time for many families. Parents are often tired and rushed while children are hungry and irritable. In many homes, supper is announced by Mother saying, "Get your toys picked up and wash your hands; dinner will be ready in a few minutes." Children commonly do not respond, so the next call is, "I'm putting dinner on the table. Hurry up!" If another call is ignored (particularly if Dad has not responded either), Mother usually becomes frustrated and angry. When the children finally come to the table, only to complain about the selection or to just pick at their food, the parents usually respond by nagging them to eat. This reinforces the dawdling they are trying to eliminate.

Mealtimes mean different things to children and parents. Parents look on mealtime as an opportunity for the family to talk and share their day's experiences. Children are usually hungry and are mainly interested in filling their stomachs and returning to play or television.

We recommend that parents say once that dinner is ready and then start the meal with whoever is present. After allowing a reasonable time for the meal to be completed, the table is cleared without anger or criticism. If the children are a little late at the table they will miss the opportunity to complete their meal, and if they are very late for dinner they may miss the meal completely. Remove the dinner plates from the table and tell the children that you hope they will enjoy breakfast the next morning.

How long should dinnertime be? For the child who is hyperactive with a short attention span, it may last only a few minutes. Few children can tolerate the longer mealtime parents like.

Many parents feel guilty if their child does not have a full meal, but almost all children can miss several meals without any physical harm, so their own appetite becomes a powerful incentive to arrive at the table promptly. It is all right to give your child a glass of milk before bedtime if she does not eat her dinner, but giving a half-sandwich, apple, or cookie reinforces the behavior you are trying to eliminate and should be avoided.

Many children like only a narrow range of food. Even adults do not like everything, so it is reasonable for your children to be allowed to avoid food they find objectionable. Meals should be presented to the child, who then has the option of eating or not eating. If children do not eat they wait until the next meal and experience mild hunger. If parents fix special meals for a child, they reinforce picky eating.

Throughout this book we have emphasized the importance of consistency and follow-through. This applies to mealtime problems too, including poor table manners or repeatedly leaving the table. Do not indulge and reinforce bad habits.

A child should be given one warning; if the behavior continues he should be excused from the table and sent to his room until dinner is over. Parents should be sensitive to the restlessness of a hyperactive child and excuse him in a reasonably short period, but do not allow any child to repeatedly get up and run into the living room to look at television.

We are frequently asked what is a reasonable length of time for dinner and we usually answer, "More than five minutes but not longer than an hour." Even though your daughter may rush through her meal, she should be allowed to leave after a short time. Do not force a child with ADHD to sit at the table when she is uncomfortable doing so.

BEDTIME

Some children with ADHD need less sleep than others the same age. If you think about a time when it was hard for you to fall asleep (although many mothers will find it difficult to remember any time when they have not been tired), you can understand the feeling of a child with ADHD who has been sent to bed but is not ready to go to sleep.

Children learn that they can delay bedtime by saying, "I want a drink," "I have to go to the bathroom," or "I forgot to have you sign my school permission slip." After several such stalls, many parents become frustrated and angrily enforce bedtime, causing parent and child to separate for the night upset with each other. Sometimes these delaying behaviors work and children learn that success results from persistence.

At the end of the day, adults need time to rest, wind down, and recover. Most parents feel they are still "on duty" while the children are up. We find it helpful to enforce a strict time for the child to be in his room, but to allow him to play quietly, read, or listen to the radio until he naturally falls asleep. Do not try to force your child to sleep; you cannot, so it only leads to frustration for everyone.

A Sleep Bank is helpful. First, set the time you want your child in her room; this is not the time she starts getting ready for bed. Many parents start their child toward bed early because they know that there are delaying actions ahead. The final bedtime should be explained as the time when the last question has been asked, the last kiss given, the last prayer said, the last trip made to the bathroom, and the last drink finished.

Give your child the option of deciding when he wants to start getting ready for bed. One child may choose to prepare for bed in a more leisurely fashion and start earlier; another may choose to do it more quickly and use less time. Every minute the child is up after the final bedtime is a minute that has to be paid back to the Sleep Bank the next night. If your child goes to bed 5 minutes late, the next night she goes to bed 5 minutes earlier. If she gets up to ask a question 25 minutes after bedtime, she pays 25 minutes to the Sleep Bank the next night.

It is seldom necessary to use the Sleep Bank more than two or three nights before the child accepts the new routine and goes to bed with fewer delays. A child can be told that he can stay up until his new bedtime but if he has to pay back time to the Sleep Bank it is because of a decision he made the previous night. Since the time is always paid back the next night, consequences never carry over or become excessive.

PUBLIC BEHAVIOR

Troublesome behavior in public or in automobiles is the most difficult behavior to change. Management strategies available at home are usually not accessible when children are in public. We encourage parents to think of behavioral problems away from home as occurring in two types of settings—public places, such as stores, malls, and restaurants, and the homes of friends or relatives.

Shopping can be torture for children with ADHD. Their attention span is short, their activity level is high, and they quickly become bored and disinterested. This can only mean further upset and stress for both parents and their child. Make it easy for yourself and your child; do not take her places where it is likely that she will act up. Trade babysitting with a neighbor so your child can be spared an experience that may lead to anger and tears for all involved.

If you must take your child shopping and he acts up, set limits quickly and effectively. While consequences can be applied after you have returned home, they are less effective because of the delay between the behavior and the time when the consequences are applied. For example, if you are eating in a fast-food restaurant and your child's behavior becomes unmanageable, remove him immediately. While you may leave uneaten food on the table, you will impress your child with the fact that you are ready to do what it takes to impose limits regardless of where you are. On the other hand, if your child acts up when you are shopping, you may encourage further problems by removing him from a situation he did not want to be in in the first place. In the restaurant example, your child is not allowed to finish a meal he presumably wants, whereas removing him from a store may give him exactly what he does want. Promising your children an extra treat after the completion of a successful shopping trip may be helpful, but nothing works better than keeping the trip short and avoiding shopping with your child whenever possible.

When you and your child visit other people's houses, you should use the same management techniques you would use at home. It can be embarrassing to discipline a child when you are visiting, but doing so will significantly reduce the likelihood of the behavior happening again.

Children are often selective about when they cause trouble. For example, they may do so in one grandparent's home, but not in another's. This is because they sense that parents will often be less tolerant of their acting up and will impose stricter limits in one home than in the other. Isolation can be almost as effective in a friend's or relative's home as in your own.

Car travel can be difficult for children with ADHD because of their short attention span and hyperactivity. Few techniques work well, but planning only short trips or providing games and activities can reduce their frustration. If their behavior gets out of control, stop the car and tell your children that you will not start again until they are quiet.

MANAGING YOUR CHILD'S ROOM

Conflict over the cleanliness of children's rooms is common. If you remember your own childhood, you will realize that housekeeping is often quite different for children than for adults. There is no relationship between how children maintain their rooms and adult standards for cleanliness and hygiene. Occasionally, children who are held to very strict standards of neatness rebel as adults and live in messy houses, while others continue to be neat. Likewise, messy children often change dramatically when they have their own home and become clean and orderly. Parents rarely win a power struggle over keeping a neat room. If a child is determined to resist her parents' requests for orderliness, there will always be one more sock or piece of underwear under the bed to irritate you. As in so many similar situations, parents become more frustrated and controlling and children become more resistant and defiant.

We have found that parents have the least conflict with their children over room management when they establish natural consequences and avoid a power struggle. Parents become frustrated when they insist that a room be kept a certain way, get no cooperation from their child, and find that their efforts to keep the room clean are being interfered with. What parent does not get frustrated digging dirty clothes from underneath the bed? We suggest that parents tell children that their room is a personal living area and they have the right to keep it as they like. Along with the opportunity for a child to keep his room as he wishes goes the responsibility of caring for his clothes and his room.

As adults, you anticipate the clothes you will need and then make sure that they are available. It is reasonable for children and teenagers to assume the same responsibility. We suggest that you tell your children that you will no longer go into their rooms to collect dirty clothes; clothes will only be washed if the children put them into the proper receptacle on washing day. Later, as they grow older, you may want to switch full responsibility for laundry to the children. Wash whatever clothes are in the designated location and return them to your children's rooms. Initially, most children will not anticipate their laundry needs and will find themselves without jeans, socks, or underwear. You can be supportive and remind the children that everything in the designated location was washed. On the next washing day you will be happy to take care of whatever needs to be done then. Going without a special pair of jeans or underwear for a day is a minor natural consequence, but one that will emphasize the need for the children to assume responsibility for their own clothes. Usually, children quickly conform to such a system and are happier with it; this reduces parents' frustration.

Parents can either tell their children where the clean sheets are so they can change their own beds or put fresh bed linens in a child's room after an appropriate interval. If the child wants the bed changed, she can do it herself.

When the room becomes unsightly, as it surely will, parents should close the door so they will not have to see it when they walk by. Usually rooms deteriorate for a time until even the child is no longer comfortable with the dishevelment and it is cleaned up, but not always. Sometimes the mess remains. Children rarely keep their rooms as their parents would like, or as they will when they become adults. Since it is their living area, they should feel in control of it. Avoid this absolutely unnecessary conflict and your relationship with your child will improve.

One note of caution. Many children with ADHD are so disorganized that they need some extra help to get things done. Be alert to your child's need for help, but be sure to distinguish their need for help from your own need to force your child to comply with your expectations for his room. Special attention may have to be given to supervision of a work-study area in which schoolwork can be done.

HOW MUCH FREEDOM IS ENOUGH?

As children get older they need and want greater independence. How much freedom to allow a child is a question that arises in every family but that is usually of greater concern to parents of a child with ADHD. It is natural for parents of children with ADHD not to allow freedom for their children because "they are not mature enough to handle it." There is often truth to this assessment, but if children are not allowed to learn by experiencing the natural consequences of their behavior, they will never be able to manage their own lives. The children and adolescents who need the most practice in solving the problems of living get the least experience. Eventually children reach the age where they will demand or just take their autonomy but they may not have had the same opportunity to learn as others their age. Allow your child with ADHD the opportunity to learn about life by experiencing it so she will be ready for the responsibilities of adulthood.

Parents who are concerned about their child's safety may respond not only to the reality of a potentially dangerous situation but also to their own feelings of vulnerability. With careful thought, most parents can become aware of how their own feelings and fears affect their treatment of their children. When this proves difficult, professional help may be needed.

Equally important in the development of their child's behavior is the role of the parents' personalities. Most parents raise their children the way they were raised even if they were dissatisfied with that approach. Others may go to the opposite extreme; if they were raised by very strict parents they may commit themselves to a more permissive approach. Child management research shows that children raised in either very strict or very lenient homes have more problems than those raised in moderate homes. It is interesting that children reared in homes with either very strict rules or few or no rules both usually end up more oppositional and defiant. Children from more authoritarian homes tend to internalize anger and rage at what they perceive to be unfair treatment and then project and displace these feelings onto those around them. Children raised more permissively do not learn acceptable rules or standards of behavior and behave in ways that please themselves but cause difficulty for others. Much of our work with parents involves helping them avoid either extreme. Many parents know that this middle-of-the-road approach is reasonable but have difficulty implementing it. The parents' own personalities and attitudes about themselves usually get in the way.

Parents want the best for their children and hope that they will avoid some of the pitfalls the parents experienced. Parents enjoy seeing their children do well and normally feel bad when children fail or are unhappy. If parents are unable to view their children as separate entities instead of extensions of themselves, they will find it difficult to avoid forcing their own values onto their children. Encouraging age-appropriate autonomy is a good vaccine against any psychological problems and reduces power struggles between parents and children.

One of the most important developmental tasks of adolescence is to establish a separate identity. Failure to do this usually means that the child will be unsure of himself or will be passive and dependent as an adult. If parents do not allow a child to separate and establish a separate identity, the implication is that they will continue to approve of or influence all of the child's future decisions, who he dates, where he attends college, what kind of job he will take, who he marries, where he lives, and how he raises his children. Few adults could tolerate that kind of controlling relationship, and yet some parents impose exactly this situation on their own children.

Parents usually do what they think is in their child's best interest, but if their own self-concept is so poor that they cannot tolerate separate behavior, conflict may arise. It is sometimes necessary for parents to love their children enough to allow them to make mistakes and experience the natural consequences of their behavior. Sometimes parents who feel that they will lose control of their children become overly strict in an attempt to prevent this from happening. This approach rarely works because all children eventually take their autonomy and the only question is not "if" but "how" and "when."

Parents may also fear losing the love of their child and feel that they can only maintain their child's affection by acquiescing to their every demand. When children become aware of this feeling, they use it to manipulate their parents.

At one time or another, most children tell their parents they hate them. It is said in anger and quickly forgotten. If parents fear their child's disapproval they may foolishly do anything to forestall their child's anger at any cost; this fosters manipulative behavior.

AGGRESSION

Children with ADHD are often aggressive or may appear so. They lack the ability to stop and recognize the implications of their actions, so they say and do things that appear to be aggressive but are actually only evidence of their impulsivity. They usually recognize that they have behaved badly, but they do not know how to control themselves. Think how often you pause before saying something because it may be misunderstood or offensive, or how you hesitate before climbing on a chair to reach a high shelf because you realize that the chair is unsteady and you may fall.

There are also other causes of aggression. Research shows that aggression is influenced by several factors that can be controlled. Children learn more from watching what others do than in any other way. How much of your behavior is a result of watching the way other people act, talk, dress, or behave and then imitating the models you like? Therefore, parents who are either verbally or physically aggressive are actually sending the message: "If someone is doing something you don't like, yell at them or hit them!" The people we love and admire most are the ones who are the most effective models. Your children love you more than anyone in the world, so it should come as no surprise that you will be their most influential model. How you handle frustration, differences of opinion with your spouse, and common household problems will provide your children with the model they will adopt.

As we have mentioned before, physical punishment has many undesirable side effects; one of the most important is that it shows your child that it is all right to hit people when she is unhappy. It should come as no surprise that children who tend to be more impulsive and aggressive often begin to hit siblings, peers, and even parents as they grow older. One of the important rules in reducing aggressive behavior in your child is to be sure that you do not model it!

Another important factor influencing aggression is how much the aggressor is rewarded for his behavior. Research shows that each time a child is successfully aggressive and does not experience a consequence for it, the probability is increased that he will become even more aggressive. It is therefore important that when your child with ADHD is aggressive he experience some immediate nonaggressive consequences, such as isolation, in order to learn that his aggression is neither tolerated nor successful.

We also know that the more nurturance your child receives, the less likely it is that she will be aggressive. The more your child is loved, supported, and treated with kindness, the less likely it is that she will demonstrate aggression. We all want to care for our children this way, but it is sometimes hard when your child is hyperactive or impulsive; yet this is the child who particularly needs all the patience and love we can provide.

We are often asked about the effect of television on children's aggressive behavior. Approximately 90% of children are not significantly affected by watching aggressive behavior and do not become more aggressive as a result of seeing it on television. Another 10% are significantly affected by watching aggressive, violent television. Children with ADHD are more likely to appear in this latter group. If your child has a tendency toward aggression, do what you can to limit his television watching of aggressive programs. The least desirable programs are those in which violence is portrayed as a real-life event, while the least damaging is violence pictured in cartoons. The less violence and aggression your children see on television, the less likely they will be to act aggressively.

Preventing Problems at Home

The emotional swings of a child with ADHD are hard on the whole family. Everyone has to make a continuing effort to prevent problems rather than scolding or punishing after the event. Mastering the ideas presented in this chapter will help you live harmoniously with your youngster with ADHD.

There are several reasons why it is more difficult to discipline a child with ADHD. First, no matter how sophisticated the parent is, it is impossible to be certain whether troublesome behavior reflects ADHD symptoms or habits learned along the way. Consequently, the disciplinarian is always in the position of being uncertain about how strict to be, how much to ignore, and what expectations to have when dealing with other children in the family.

Second, it is often hard to be sure whether you are having any effect on a child with ADHD. When an average child misbehaves from time to time, a few stern words, occasional punishment, and reasonable consistency will usually bring the behavior into line. A similar strategy will work to some extent with a child who has ADHD, but because of the child's poor impulse control and emotional lability, behavioral problems are constantly renewed. The disciplinarian may wonder whether she is having any impact on the child.

Many traditional notions of child rearing have to be set aside or modified. Consider the example of giving your child responsibility for taking the garbage out to the street once a week. If you have already tried this, you will recognize your family in the following descriptions. No matter how many times you ask your son to take a garbage can or a plastic bag to the street on a certain day or at a certain time, it never seems to get done. If you raise your voice or ask him to do it this minute and then supervise him, he will usually do it; any other technique does not work. In fact, most parents say that their child will trip and fall over the garbage 10 times and still walk past it without carrying it to the street.

What is a parent to do? Keep in mind that most children do not set out to be defiant. Their inability to follow through on a simple task like this does not reflect serious psychological problems or even a problem in their relationship with you. Your youngster with ADHD, like most children, probably intends to do it right. When he sees the garbage, he means to take it out to the street; then his mind usually jumps to something else. If he thinks about the garbage at all, he probably tells himself that he will get back to it in a moment. Of course, that moment never comes and the job never gets done.

You have to make a decision. First, decide what you want to accomplish. If your goal is to get the garbage to the street, that is one thing. If your goal is to teach your child to do it responsibly, on his own, every week at a certain time, that is a different goal; if you have the latter goal, you are probably in trouble. If you want the garbage taken out to the street, gently tell your child the next time the garbage is ready, "Son, the garbage here has to be taken out to the street, and we'd like you to do it right now, because if you don't it might not get done." With this approach, you are going to have the responsibility every week of organizing this task for your child.

If, like most parents, you say, "But when will he learn to take responsibility himself?" you are focusing on the wrong aspect of the problem. Your child with ADHD is probably no more irresponsible than any other child. Unfortunately, the symptoms of ADHD create behaviors and habits that often look like irresponsibility or bad attitudes but are not. These behavioral problems require creative, careful, constructive planning to ensure that the work gets done, the child has a feeling of satisfaction about a job well done, and parents do not feel exploited or helpless.

It is best to prevent problems rather than dealing with them after they occur. Guiding your child to the street with the garbage prevents the confrontation over why he did not do it. In most cases the key to prevention is to avoid situations that produce problems in the first place. It also is not possible to prevent all problems; you have to prepare for things that cannot be avoided. Learn to recognize impending emotional upset. Analyze when your child is likely to get upset and think of ways to forestall these situations. If, for example, your daughter gets into trouble just before dinner, perhaps she should eat dinner earlier or have a bigger after-school snack. Trouble late in the evening may mean that she should go to bed earlier.

You can see that suggestions of this type, when applied to your child, may require major alterations in your family routine. You may not like doing this. You may resent all the extra effort for a child who already has created more than his fair share of family trouble. The decision is yours. The important point we want to make is that this is an essential part of living with a youngster with ADHD. The resulting peace of mind and tranquility are worth the extra effort.

ADHD is a physical handicap and has to be recognized as such, although it is not a visible handicap. If your child limped because one leg was shorter than the other, and consequently he could not win races, you would not punish him, call him a bad boy, or tell him he was an irresponsible athlete. Yet many parents blame their child with ADHD when his failure to control his impulses or to organize and coordinate his own activities causes him continually to fail to take out the garbage or complete his homework. Some regard his problem behavior as a reflection of a deficiency of character or attitude that can be remedied with harsh criticism.

Try to avoid confrontations over trivial matters. You can find a dividing line between letting your child get away with small things that trouble you and giving her so much freedom that she learns bad habits or does not learn proper behaviors.

Children with ADHD seem to fall apart over unexpected changes in plans. This usually means careful preparation for changes in routine. It involves several explanations about what is going to happen that another child may not require. Recognize that unexpected changes of plans may cause more disruption in the life of your child with ADHD, and direct your efforts toward settling him down rather than criticizing him for his overreaction.

Always be on guard to avoid confrontations and trouble unless the issue is essential. This is not easy advice to follow. It requires a strong commitment and a lot of practice. Some parents get upset when they hear this advice because they fear that they might teach their children bad habits this way. If it is carefully done, that will not happen. It is more important to keep things calm than it is to seize every small opportunity to show your child that she is not living up to your expectations.

NONPUNITIVE DISCIPLINE

Parents and educators face a daily challenge to find strict disciplinary techniques that do not frustrate the child or injure his already fragile self-esteem. We must constantly search for ways to ally ourselves with our children against these problems.

The best method is to seek ways of allowing your child to face the natural consequences of behavior. Take, as an example, a 10-year-old boy who repeatedly fails to put his bicycle in the garage in the evening. His father becomes increasingly annoyed, fearing that he may drive over the bike because he cannot see it and worried that the bike might be stolen. Everyone has a similar personal example. How many times do you remind your child of the dangers to his bicycle? How many times do you explain before he will catch on?

Natural consequences teach best. Explain the problem to your child. Explain the risks he is taking. Then stop. We explain too many things to our children too many times—especially if they seem to ignore us. The problem is rarely that you have not been heard or understood.

Now, imagine that the bike is stolen; what do you do then? Remember, the child is going to be angry and upset and may be to blame. In our experience, parents make an unfortunate decision at this point far too often. They see this as an opportunity to finally hammer home the lesson that the child's negligence caused the bike to be lost. The child knows it is his fault, of course. Even a 10-year-old of average intelligence can understand that the bike was stolen as a natural consequence of his own behavior. We want him to understand that. However, if you view this as an opportunity to teach the same old lesson, your child has only two ways of dealing with his troubled feelings.

He may feel so guilty and inadequate that your lecture strips him of his remaining self-esteem and makes him feel worse about himself. He has all that anger and hurt bottled up inside because his bicycle is gone. When you jump in with your blame and recriminations you become a tempting target for his anger and blame, instead of helping him to examine his own behavior to see where he went wrong.

The same pattern occurs time and time again in the life of the 15-year-old who brings home a report card with failing grades. She may feel angry, frustrated, bewildered, and, although she does not show it, hurt by those grades. If you choose that moment to be critical, you become a lightning rod for her misery and an easy target for blame. Your teenager says to you, "The reason I get these bad grades is because you're on my back all the time. If you'd leave me alone, I would do better."

Let us take a closer look at two unnecessary and potentially harmful things that happen in these circumstances. First, the child is denied an opportunity to take a critical look at his own behavior and learn from it. It is true, of course, that the child is his own worst enemy. He is the one who may refuse to examine his own behavior. Heaven knows, you have been trying long enough to keep him out of trouble. Nonetheless, the child's failings should not blind you to the critical role you play when you respond to such problems in a harsh, critical, or rejecting manner.

The second unfortunate consequence in these situations is the lost opportunity for an adult to establish an alliance with the child against the problem. This alliance keeps the adult-child relationship strong and positive. It helps the child fight some of the frustration, bewilderment, and loss of self-esteem that inevitably occur.

Children often do a good job of hiding their feelings. We have heard parents say again and again, "What she does wouldn't be so bad if only it seemed as if she cared." While a minority of children truly do not care about their own behavior or its effect on others, the majority care desperately. Because they feel helpless, they learn to hide their feelings and build a superficial shell around themselves. They hope to protect themselves from the outside world and preserve their dignity and self-respect.

Life often harshly punishes children with ADHD. Isn't losing a bike punishment enough? What, then, is an alternative response to a child with ADHD? We will offer several examples of responses to similar situations. We want to emphasize that these are not gimmicks to be applied to isolated problems. Establishing an alliance with your child to work together on problems must reflect a genuine commitment on your part. This must include recognition that ADHD is a chronic problem that invades every corner of a child's life. The most practical help you can provide goes well beyond solving day-to-day problems. Your efforts must make clear to your child that you understand the problem, you do not blame the child for his handicap, and you will work together, despite the continuing frustration you both experience.

Return to the stolen bicycle. The wise parent holds his tongue and resists the temptation to remind the child that he would not have this problem if he had listened to your advice. Instead, go to your child, put your arm around his shoulder, and let him know you understand how bad he feels about the loss of the bicycle. Tell him that you share his frustration and feelings of loss. Say, "I know how important your bike was to you. If you want me to, I'll help you save up money to buy another. I have several ideas about how you can earn some money, and there are extra chores around the house we will pay you for."

You must be sincere. These are not clever words to be used to manipulate your son. He will still be upset. He will not greet what you say with joy. But if you approach the problem this way, you establish a partnership with your child. If he still is tempted to blame you or refuses to accept responsibility for his own behavior, let it pass without comment. Follow through with support and positive emphasis to prevent the more serious consequence of having your child identify you as part of the problem.

If you follow this advice, do not expect your son to suddenly turn over a new leaf and always remember to put his possessions away safely. After all, this is not a memory problem in the first place. Nor will he "learn" his lesson. This is not a learning problem. He will simply be better able to profit from the experience because you have kept your conflict out of the problem arena. You have not muddied the water with other issues. If you follow through with other, less dramatic and less clear-cut examples in the same way, a pattern will eventually be established that will allow your child to grow and gain self-understanding, in addition to strengthening your relationship.

Such a "nonintervention" strategy has to be applied with good judgment. While it may be appropriate to allow a 10-year-old child to suffer the natural consequences of a stolen bicycle, we cannot let the same child face alone the consequences of her failure to complete schoolwork. We have already addressed the issue of helping with homework. By the time a child is 15 years old, however, there is little that parents or teachers can do to force her to do her schoolwork. Each case must be decided based on the parents' knowledge of their child. You may reach a point where the same careful steps must be taken to allow a teenager to face the natural consequences of her behavior in school. This may mean failing a course, being suspended from school, or even being dismissed from school for a semester. As unfortunate and regrettable as these may be, they are often preferable to getting involved in destructive fights and arguments at home. If you choose to fight, you may inflame things further. Then, if a child fails or drops out of school, relationships with teachers and parents have become so strained that the child finds it difficult to recover and resume her education. Keep your eye on your goals. Today's exam grade may be less important than a child's opinion about herself or her overall attitude toward education.

We were impressed with the behavior of the assistant principal in one local high school. He was responsible for attendance and discipline. His management of all students, with and without problems, was characterized by firmness and consistency. For example, the school had a rule that allowed five unexcused absences per term. If a child exceeded that number, he was dropped from the class. There were no exceptions. Equally important, there was no additional punishment in the form of school restrictions or criticism. Parents were counseled and were encouraged to be supportive and urge their children to attend class and complete their assignments, but not to add additional punishment if a student was dismissed from class.

This man's approach to his students was honest and straightforward. He could look a student in the eye or put his hand on a boy's shoulder and say, "You're having a problem getting to class. You've exceeded the five unexcused absences and are being dropped from that class. I'm here to help you. If you want to work out something with me to make sure you can get to the rest of your classes this semester, or if next term you need my help keeping to a schedule, let me know." He was always available. If he saw a student he had disciplined a few days before, he would talk to her, be supportive, and indicate his availability to help without being overbearing.

Many students credited this man's method of dealing with attendance and other discipline problems as being the reason they did not develop an overall negative attitude toward school that would affect them later in life. A number of students from that school have been our patients. They have told us how this sort of experience made them willing to take another chance on school later or made them feel that it was worth trying a course again the next semester.

Some parents and teachers may be alarmed at our suggestion that they not put up a stronger fight to keep a child in class or in school. But after fighting, arguing, threatening, disciplining, grounding, crying, and grinding your teeth, recognize that more may be gained by allowing your child to face the natural consequences of his behavior and establishing an alliance with him against the problem than there is by continuing with useless and potentially destructive confrontations.

SCHEDULES

Scheduling your child's activities is often helpful. Like other advice we have offered, this too requires time and effort. In scheduling activities and free time, you have to consider your child's impulsivity and inability to organize things himself. Young children with ADHD often benefit from a schedule like the following:

3:00—Arrive home from school, have milk and cookies

3:15—Do homework

3:30—Go outside to play ball

4:00—Do homework

4:15—Practice piano

4:30—Go outside to play

5:30—Read

And so forth.

This sort of schedule does not work as well with older children because you cannot control them as effectively. Notice that there are longer periods, and more total time, for play than for homework and practicing piano. This takes into consideration the child's limited attention span and lower threshold of frustration. Of course, you are going to have to enforce the schedule. It is a way of getting things done so homework is not still hanging over the child's head at suppertime and parents are not facing the evening with dread, wondering what kind of fight will be caused by their insistence that the child do 15 minutes' worth of homework or practice the piano.

Schedules have to be fairly strict and, at the same time, incorporate flexibility. On some days there will be no homework, and sometimes there will be other activities to add to the schedule. If a child can read, the schedule should be written. Post it on the door of the refrigerator, the bulletin board, or a wall in her room. Post several copies. The written schedule helps focus the child's attention. If it is written, she can look at the schedule to see what has to be done. This helps organize her activities and makes it clearer and less confusing for her than carrying the schedule around in her head.

This idea of writing things down for children with ADHD can be applied in other areas. The more concrete and explicit these areas are, the more notes and schedules will add to the child's ability to organize his activities and understand what is expected of him at different times of the day, and the better he will be able to meet those expectations.

For the child with ADHD, the value of getting homework completed and getting good grades is not only that he did the work, but that he can take satisfaction in the accomplishment. Life is full of failure and frustration for your child. Every time you create a successful experience for him, you go a long way toward counteracting the negative effects of all the bad things that happen so often.

REMOVING A CHIP ON THE SHOULDER

Parents frequently say that their child has a chip on her shoulder. They mean that she seems to be looking for a fight. As one mother expressed it, "It doesn't seem to matter what you say to her when she's in one of those moods; it's always the wrong thing to say."

This attitude comes from a self-esteem problem. Children with ADHD usually lack confidence because experiences prove that they do not do things well. This robs them of self-confidence, lowers their self-esteem, and makes them overly sensitive. Because of this oversensitivity, they readily interpret, or even misinterpret, even the most gentle things you say as criticism.

For example, your son may be watching television by himself, selecting the programs he wants without concern for anyone else. After 3 hours, his sister comes into the room and asks to see a particular channel. An argument starts and you try to intervene. It is reasonable to say to your son, "Your sister should have a turn; you've been watching TV for the past 3 hours."

Why in the world should something so reasonable cause him to explode? The answer is not in what you said; it is in understanding your son. He has a long memory filled with many examples of times he has been criticized and treated in ways he thinks unfair. If your family is typical, he thinks his sister always is given more privileges than he is and gets away with a lot more than he does. He is so sensitive to this issue that any time you criticize him in favor of his sister, even when you are being fair and reasonable, he is not thinking about this one time; he immediately feels salt rubbed in the old wound of his sister being treated better than he is. That is why you see a strong reaction from him. It may seem unreasonable to you, but that is not going to change the way things are.

How do you respond? What do you do? Some of his outbursts must be ignored. If you are satisfied that your expectations are fair and reasonable, enforce the rule. If your son makes a fuss, send him out of the room, assuming that he has not already stomped out in a rage.

Do not try to explain the logic of your decision then. He will not be listening. His feelings are not governed by the same logic you use. His view of the situation is so different from yours that it is impossible to have a commonsense discussion with him then. Later, after he has settled down, try to explain your actions to him. Explain the fairness of what happened. Also explain to him your understanding that he felt unfairly treated compared to his sister, and say that you know it was part of his reaction over the TV.

Doing as we have suggested will not eliminate the problem. It will happen again and again. It will also occur in other circumstances. The positive effect will come from letting your child know you understand him, even if he is not able to express these feelings and ideas himself. It will keep this episode from being part of the large collection of injustices he has already collected and used as proof of how badly he is treated. If you can prevent him from adding further to this collection, you will make him feel a little more valued, a little less rejected, and a little more a part of the family. This becomes one small increment added to many other small increments you put together to make modest, but significant, changes in your child's behavior. Eventually, there will be a reduction in the frequency and intensity of outbursts in similar situations.

Most parents find advice of this kind useful and are able to follow through on it. A problem arises when there are no immediate or dramatic changes in a child's behavior. It is easy to slip back into bad habits and feelings of discouragement, which cause you to give up efforts that do not seem to have a payoff. Our discussion of how behavior is learned and the value of reinforcers applies to you as well. If you do not get a reward or a reinforcement for something you are doing, such as working constructively to change your child's behavior, why should you keep at it?

You must work to be your own reinforcer. Mother and father have to work together to reinforce each other. Early on, when you first try some of the ideas in this book, you will get no reward other than to say to yourself, "Well, I guess I feel a little less upset because I know I'm doing the right thing." Another reward worth a great deal comes when your spouse pats you on the shoulder, gives you a hug, and says, "I think you handled that very well." That ought to hold you for a while. Eventually you will begin to see the tension in your house lessen and note improvements in your child's relationships with brothers, sisters, and other children.

Patience and persistence, Mother. Patience and persistence, Father. Find your reinforcers where you can. It can be a long and difficult road raising a child with ADHD. It is, however, possible to do it in a constructive, mentally healthy way that will provide rich rewards for you and your child.

Parents often have concern about the effect of the behavior of a child with ADHD on other children in the family. They worry that siblings may pick up bad habits by mimicking the behavior of their brothers or sisters with ADHD. They also fear the effect on their other children of the extra time and attention the child with ADHD demands.

How serious a problem is this and is there a solution?

In the course of our work with children with ADHD and their families, parents tell of their concern: "I am worried about Annie," one mother said. "She is only 2 years old but she is beginning to pick up a lot of Billy's behaviors. Now, when I ask her to do something, I see the same angry defiance in her face and the same stubbornness when she refuses to give in. I don't think I can take two children like that."

Children in the same family will use the behavior of a sibling as a model. Children do pick up bad habits from each other. Fortunately, the problem is not as serious as it may first appear.

In a family counseling session, Debbie, the 15-year-old sister of Dan, who has ADHD, asked her parents, "Why do you get on my case every time I'm 5 minutes late coming home or don't tell you where I'm going to be after school? Last week Danny didn't come home until 4 o'clock in the morning and nothing happened to him."

Debbie's parents responded to her appropriately. They told her that they were pleased with her behavior and they acknowledged that she was responsible, reliable, and gave them no cause for mistrust. Debbie's mother went on to explain that the family had the same rules for her as they had for Danny and their older brother. The fact that Danny had a problem and the family was less successful in getting him to stick to those rules in no way changed their expectations that the other two children would abide by them.

The parents refused to allow themselves to be drawn into a discussion of what is fair. They continued to emphasize to all three of their children that just because Danny broke the rules did not mean that they were going to allow the other two to run free so everyone would be equal.

Avoid arguments with your children about what is fair. We certainly believe that children should be treated with respect. We also believe that they should be allowed to participate in establishing rules and guidelines for responsible behavior. Nonetheless, families are not democracies. Everyone should not have an equal vote. There are times when parents must assert their authority.

One family we know handled this well. They had three children, and from the time the children were very young the parents tried to make sure the children did not manipulate them or catch them in arguments about what was fair. For example, if a cookie or a slice of cake had to be divided into three pieces for the children, the parents would not tolerate any discussion about who got the bigger piece.

The children's mother told us, "I would always tell them that it was impossible for me to divide a cookie into three equal parts. I would try to be fair, but sometimes somebody would get a bigger piece and there was nothing I could do about it. I told them that it would all average out by the time they were 18, but in the meantime I did not want to have any discussion about who got more."

Human beings are different and have different needs. The fairest thing to do is to treat them differently according to their needs.

Misplaced efforts to treat all your children fairly are doomed to failure. In fact, the more one child protests about his unfair treatment, the more likely it is that fairness is not the issue at all. In many families the child with ADHD protests loudest and longest that he is being treated unfairly. This is the same child who is getting more of your attention, more of your psychological energy, and more of your financial resources, and he still feels like a second-class citizen in his own family.

Protests about unfair treatment, carried to an extreme, are usually an expression of the child's diminished self-concept. The child feels so bad about herself, and considers herself so much an outsider in her own family, that she cannot look at things objectively and see that she may be getting more, not less, of everything. Frantic attempts to convince the child that everything is fair are rarely effective because they do not address the underlying issue of the child's bad feelings about herself.

Discipline for your children should be consistent with the standards and expectations you have set within your family. Although some of your children may mimic the behavior of their sister or brother with ADHD for a short time, the imposition of regular discipline with an explanation of your expectations for them will usually control their behavior.

From time to time they may be tempted to act up again; also, from time to time, resentment will build as they see what appears to be the greater leeway allowed their brother or sister. The proper response is to be consistent with your discipline and accompany it with an explanation of why you are having problems keeping your child's behavior in line. Other children in the family seldom develop serious behavioral problems because they are modeling the behavior of a brother or sister. If other children develop behavioral problems, it is often because the parents' confidence in their role as disciplinarian is shaken. They respond to the other children, and this allows the disruptive behavior to continue.

PARENTS WITH ADHD AND THEIR CHILDREN WITH ADHD

We mentioned in chapter 1 that ADHD runs in families. There is an increased likelihood that one or both parents of a child with ADHD will also have the disorder. No one has documented the precise extent of this heritability factor, but the likelihood that one parent of a child with ADHD will also have the disorder should always be considered.

The dilemma faced by families with more than one member with ADHD is substantial. In such a case we are asking a parent who may be impulsive and short-tempered or emotionally labile to be especially patient and understanding of a child with similar symptoms. The problem is more difficult because the parent frequently has not been diagnosed. Not only does the father, for example, not understand the significance of his own behavior, but the very symptoms of ADHD may create extra stress for him at work and may contribute to tension within the marriage.

Adults with ADHD may develop elaborate techniques to compensate for their problem. Without fully understanding the nature of the disorder, many adults learn to be overly organized or especially well controlled. They do this because they realize that they cannot allow themselves any room for error. Although unable to define their problem as ADHD, they know they are forgetful if they do not keep lists, disorganized if they do not keep everything carefully in place, and easily upset when things go wrong.

Consider the family with a husband and father who has learned to organize himself as a compensation for his ADHD, of which he is not even aware, and a child who has the very symptoms that threaten the structure and organization the parent struggles so desperately to protect. Expert consultation and diagnosis are essential in such cases. Understanding why people behave as they do, and where seemingly unexplainable behavior comes from, lessens tension and helps people find coping methods.

Compulsive organization is only one method of coping with ADHD. There are many others. Some are helpful and some less so. Some can be harmful. It is important for both parents of a child with ADHD to examine their own behavior to see if they might possibly have ADHD. If so, it may be a good idea to get professional consultation for themselves.

THE NEED FOR PSYCHOTHERAPY

How do you decide whether psychotherapy will be helpful for your child with ADHD or your family? Most children with ADHD do not require extensive psychological treatment. Nonetheless, many families find it immensely helpful to have several consultation sessions with a knowledgeable child psychologist to gain a better understanding of the disorder. This helps the child and other family members determine how ADHD symptoms cause behavioral and learning difficulties.

It is our practice to meet several times with the child with ADHD and other family members after the diagnosis has been made. This gives us an opportunity to discuss practical, day-to-day concerns and explain how behavioral patterns and family relationships within the family are related to, and affected by, the disorder. We find that limited counseling is sufficient for many families. With increased knowledge and understanding, families are able to work together for everyone's benefit.

A substantial number of people require more extensive psychotherapy. Psychological treatment is not directed toward the ADHD itself, which is a physical problem that is not changed by counseling or other psychological techniques. When extensive psychological treatment is required, it is often because the family relationships are so damaged that they cannot heal by themselves, even with the added understanding of the nature of the ADHD.

The child may require individual psychological treatment because of emotional problems that have developed as a result of having ADHD. Self-esteem problems are common. In some cases they are so severe that they cause depression or such discouragement with school and social relationships that the child withdraws or finds other self-destructive ways of dealing with her anguish. ADHD can also cause crippling anxiety. Many children with the disorder need help overcoming their frustration and anger.

Whether a child or family needs extensive psychotherapy or only short-term counseling, psychological assistance remains available to the family as the years go by. It is a normal feature of ADHD to encounter difficulties from time to time that the child or the family cannot solve themselves. This does not indicate that earlier psychotherapy was not effective, nor should it be taken as a sign that the child's disorder is getting worse. Rather, as children grow and enter different developmental stages, and as families change and mature, the nature of the family relationships and the demands made on individuals change. A temporary increase in psychological symptoms in the child with ADHD or troubles in family relationships may result. In some instances more extensive psychological treatment is required, but usually these problems can be managed by several counseling sessions with a child or family psychologist. The goal is to get the child and family back on the right track.

Choose a child psychologist carefully. Not all psychologists are interested in or experienced with ADHD. Your physician will normally know of other community professionals who can provide high-quality care. If you are still uncertain, do not hesitate to make inquiries of your own. Call and ask to speak to the psychologist. Explain that you have a child with ADHD. Describe the problems you are having. Ask directly whether the psychologist is experienced in these matters and thinks he or she can help you. Psychologists are not offended by such questions. On the contrary, they are welcomed because they enable the psychologists to offer their services in areas where they can be most effective.

TREATMENT OF ADULTS WITH ADHD

Many factors complicate psychological treatment of adults with ADHD. The greatest barrier to treatment is the fact that most adults are not aware that they have the problem. It is rare for adults to ask their physician for a referral to a specialist for evaluation of ADHD. It is equally rare for a family practitioner or other primary care physician to recognize the symptoms of ADHD in adults.

One reason the symptoms of ADHD go unrecognized is because, until recently, it was commonly believed that people outgrew ADHD in early adolescence. Consequently, most adult-care physicians may never have heard of hyperactivity, attention deficit disorder, or attention deficit–hyperactivity disorder or learned to recognize the symptoms or treatments for the disorder.

Those adults diagnosed as hyperactive during childhood were probably told that they would outgrow the disorder. Consequently, adults may recognize in themselves symptoms similar to those they had as children and teenagers without realizing that these symptoms are characteristic of ADHD.

During the past several years a number of reports discussing ADHD in adults have been published in medical and psychology journals as well as in magazines and newspapers. It takes a long time for this information to become established in the practice of doctors who are in a position to diagnose an adult with ADHD and offer treatment. Diagnosis of ADHD in an adult can be difficult. Even after suspicion has been raised, the possibility of the diagnosis confirming the presence of ADHD is often uncertain. The same barriers to diagnosis of ADHD in children and adolescents exist for adults.

Remember, a diagnosis of ADHD is based primarily on the pattern of an individual's behavior. The older the person, the more complex his experiences and the more likely that a particular behavior or habit might have a variety of causes. Imagine a tangled ball of yarn with many strands. Hold the end of one piece and, just by looking at the lump of yarn, try to trace the path through all the twists and turns to its other end. It is more difficult to trace the strands of behavior through the complexities of a person's life to see where they came from.

Despite this difficulty, it is usually possible to make the diagnosis of ADHD with a reasonable degree of certainty. Proper treatment depends on many factors.

We begin with education. As with children, the starting place is making sure that the adult with ADHD thoroughly understands it. This is equally important for other family members. Understanding the problem will not lead directly to complete symptom relief, but, in our experience, there is nothing more powerful in influencing marital relationships and the way people with ADHD feel about themselves than to understand why they act as they do and run into the difficulties they do throughout life.

Understanding the symptoms of ADHD may explain why you have continued as an adult to encounter frustration in work and in relationships. This understanding may help explain why high motivation has not enabled you to gain a promotion, take a college course, complete some other aspect of your education, or change how you get along with people.

Understanding that your spouse's disorganization, short attention span, and poor impulse control are the basis of some of his or her most annoying habits certainly will not change those annoying behaviors, but they will appear in a different light. Your husband's failure to follow through with responsibilities around the house will no longer appear to be an indication of his lack of concern or commitment to you and the family. You will recognize the behavior as a symptom of ADHD.

Your wife's inability to complete her high school education or her disorganized management of the house will no longer appear as reflections of her lack of intelligence, inadequacy, or failure as a wife and mother. You will recognize them as symptoms of the disorganization resulting from short attention span, distractibility, and poor impulse control.

Understanding that many of your family relationship problems are not a result of flaws in your feelings or lack of caring about each other reduces conflict and bad feelings. Many couples, after one has been diagnosed with ADHD, say that they no longer view their relationship as an adversarial one. They no longer interpret their spouse's behavior as willful and directed against them. Instead, they are able to form an alliance to work together against the symptoms and the problems that arise. This may require some counseling with a psychologist, but much of it comes directly from better understanding and knowledge about ADHD.

Robert, a 38-year-old man we know, described his experience prior to recognizing his ADHD. Because he was skilled in a trade, he had worked regularly, but with many interruptions, since he finished apprenticeship training. For nearly 20 years he never had difficulty getting a job, but on the other hand, he never held a job very long.

"I'd either get tired of the job and quit or they would get tired of me and lay me off or fire me," Robert said. "I had a lot of people tell me that I had the potential to be a very good worker because I knew what I was doing, but I didn't seem motivated."

Failure to follow through at work and a supervisor's perception that he was unmotivated should sound familiar to parents of many young people with ADHD. Of course, this man did not lack motivation; he had ADHD, which caused him to be disorganized and distractible. He frequently appeared disinterested in his work and did not give it 100% of his attention and effort.

Robert married during his 20s. Although he and his wife had a solid marriage, in many respects the same behaviors were evident at home and affected their relationship. In addition, his wife became discouraged with the pressures the frequent job changes created for the family.

As Robert approached his mid-30s he became more concerned.

"I never had trouble getting a job," he said. "As soon as I would leave one job I'd never be out of work more than a few days before I landed something else. But, as I got older, I got kind of scared because I knew that this couldn't go on forever."

The symptoms of ADHD made Robert look unreliable and unmotivated. In truth, he was a highly motivated, reliable man. He demonstrated that reliability time and time again with respect to his family responsibilities.

A talented and capable craftsperson, he always did side work along with his regular job. He knew he had to be able to count on this income because he recognized the pattern. As the years went on, there were several longer periods without a regular job. He knew the time would come when he could no longer count on readily being hired.

Robert decided to go into business for himself. Since he had been working at side jobs so long, he had a ready-made clientele. He was able to go into business and take care of himself. Coincidentally, at the same time, he was diagnosed with ADHD. Robert's diagnosis was made in conjunction with his son's evaluation and diagnosis of ADHD. This new understanding of himself allowed Robert to reassess his entire pattern of behavior.

In addition, the understanding gained from the diagnosis came as a great relief to Robert's wife. Short-term counseling helped the family. They learned the facts about ADHD and how best to deal with symptoms, and gained valuable insight into the reasons for their past family difficulties. The strain on their marriage lessened, and the management of their son's behavior improved. Robert was also able to get his wife's help in crucial areas of his new business where his ADHD symptoms made him vulnerable, such as record keeping and following through on jobs in progress.

Indications for medication of adults with ADHD are the same as for children and adolescents. First, the diagnosis must be made. You must then ask the question: To what extent is ADHD causing significant problems in the individual's life in three areas—school, work, and relationships with friends and family. If there is significant difficulty in any of these areas, medication should be considered. Medication can be very effective in treating the symptoms of ADHD in adults. About half the adults treated with either psychostimulants or antidepressants respond favorably with significant reduction in symptoms.

Because many adults first consider that they may have ADHD in conjunction with their child's evaluation or treatment for ADHD, it is tempting to use the child's medication to assess its effect on the undiagnosed parent. Do not be tempted to treat yourself, even on a trial basis, with medication prescribed for someone else. There are a number of contraindications for taking Ritalin and other drugs and only a physician can guide you.

In most cases, we prefer to see adult patients who are taking medication in psychotherapy at the same time. Psychotherapy need not be extensive. In our practice, we are currently developing group therapy programs for adults with ADHD. We have observed this same practice in other settings.

Decisions about dosage and administration of medicine must be made on an individual basis by the patient and physician. The short-acting nature of Ritalin makes possible the use of this drug on a selective basis. For example, we are familiar with one professional man whose work is quite varied. On a number of days he must sit at his desk and read large amounts of material. On other days he is primarily involved in discussions with a variety of people. He can conduct his business without the aid of medication. When he is reading, however, he is far more efficient, and can read greater amounts more effectively, when taking Ritalin.

We have also seen psychostimulants used effectively by adults taking college courses or on-the-job training programs that require the traditional academic behaviors of studying and listening to lectures and discussion.

There are other circumstances where medication for an adult might be appropriate as well. We live in the metropolitan Detroit area, where many people work in the automobile industry. We have seen Ritalin and other psychostimulants effectively used by assembly line workers who have found that they not only concentrate on their work better, but reduce their error rate and the risk of injury because they are paying attention.

Psychotherapy with an adult patient with ADHD takes many forms. Psychological treatment may be short-term with the main emphasis on helping the patient understand the nature of the disorder better. Longer-term treatment may involve extensive work with the therapist to gain a better understanding of the effect of ADHD and to examine the impact of childhood and early adult life experiences on current psychological functioning.

While poor self-concept, anxiety, and depression may all result from problems associated with symptoms of ADHD, many adults have other psychological problems that may require attention in psychotherapy.

Psychotherapy often involves a patient's spouse. Few of us live in isolation. Treatment may include marriage counseling. A patient's spouse may participate on an occasional or frequent basis to obtain maximum treatment gains.

Future Adjustment of Children with ADHD

Many parents and professionals have been pessimistic about the future of children with attention deficit–hyperactivity disorder. This pessimism, in part, reflects a lack of information about the natural cause of the disorder and frustration at not being as helpful as we want to be. Many parents view the impulsive, seemingly irresponsible behavior of their children with ADHD and become frightened as they contemplate the teenage years and adulthood. They wonder: If we have this much trouble with her as a child, what will she be like when she is a teenager? As an adult, how will she get and keep a job?

About 25% of adolescents with ADHD have problems with antisocial behavior such as fighting, occasional moderate marijuana use, and minor delinquency. Many also have failed a grade by this time, and overall their achievement is low compared to their classmates. What does the future hold for a child with ADHD?

A child with ADHD is at risk for later behavioral and psychological problems. However, there are some reassuring answers to questions about the future from the clinical experience of professionals and from the results of several follow-up studies. Many children with ADHD grow up to lead perfectly normal lives. One comprehensive study begun over 25 years ago at Children's Hospital in Montreal, Canada, provides important information. Pediatricians, psychologists, and psychiatrists studied a group of 75 children diagnosed as hyperactive. (Remember that there was no diagnosis of ADHD when the study began.) They kept in touch with the children and their families and brought them back to the hospital at regular intervals for interviews and medical and psychological testing.

The most recent report of the follow-up study was published as a book, *Hyperactive Children Grown Up*, by Gabrielle Weiss and Lily Trokenberg Hechtman (1986). The study addressed two major questions. First, how do specific symptoms of what Weiss and Hechtman called the hyperactivity syndrome (ADHD) affect life at work? Second, because it was well known that adolescents with ADHD have a relatively low self-concept, how do they fare as young adults?

There were several hundred children in the original study, and 75 were followed for 20 years into young adulthood. During that time, 10 of the 75 children had 25 or more psychotherapy sessions. The remainder had between 10 and 25 interviews with professionals for various reasons. For most, these were routine discussions with pediatricians about health and medicine. For some, these interviews included crisis management, help with particular problems as they came up, and general follow-up as they were monitored over the 20-year period. Of the 75, 65 had no elaborate psychotherapy or psychological counseling but were given advice along the way. Because the study was begun almost 30 years ago, none of the children received Ritalin. Twenty-seven of them were given the drug Thorazine®. Six received Dexedrine, 9 a mixture of drugs, and 32 no drugs at all.

The study results were based on personality tests and self-rating questionnaires. Questionnaires also were given to high school teachers and employers. The results were then compared with the results of tests given to 75 normal young adults who served as a comparison group. Because research subjects were followed over many years, it was possible to ask high school teachers the same questions that were ultimately asked of supervisors and others in a position to rate the work performance of these young adults. For instance, a teacher might be asked, "Did he get his work done?" A supervisor on the job could be asked the same question. Teachers were asked, "Would you like this person in your classroom again?" "How did he get along with his classmates?" Similarly, employers were asked, "Are you pleased you hired this person? Would you do it again?" "Does she get along with her fellow workers?" Not only was it possible to compare hyperactive young adults to nonhyperactive young adults; it also was possible to compare how these people did in the workplace with how they had done in school according to teachers' reports.

Results of the study were encouraging. There was no difference in the ratings on employer questionnaires between children with ADHD and those in the comparison group. It was also interesting to see that many of the young men and women rated satisfactorily by employers had been given poor ratings by high school teachers.

There was a difference in the teachers' ratings between hyperactive children and the comparison group. By the time the subjects went into the workplace, however, there was no difference. Looking at the mental health of the young adults classified hyperactive as children, researchers found no significant psychological disturbances in the hyperactive group. This group did tend to be more pessimistic than the comparison group and more lacking in self-confidence. They also tended to have impaired social skills.

Overall, the results of this study present some encouraging information. One important finding is that the demands of school may be different from the requirements of the workplace. Though teachers and employers both expect you to show up on time, work diligently until the job is completed, and be cooperative with co-workers, this does not seem to cause as much difficulty for the young adult on the job as it does in the last few years of high school.

About one-third to one-half of children with ADHD continued to be plagued by symptoms of the syndrome in adulthood. Problems such as antisocial behavior and drug use, as might be expected, were more common in adults who continued to have difficulty with short attention span, impulse control, and emotional lability.

We have reviewed the results of this study in some detail, because it is the most thorough, long-term project that exists and we wanted to highlight some of the encouraging features this research reports. They should be considered seriously by all who work with children with ADHD.

We must, however, stress that significant problems exist for people with ADHD and many, even those who receive excellent professional care in their early years, will continue to need some supportive psychological help as adults. Researchers Weiss and Hechtman described ADHD as a chronic, pervasive condition lasting throughout life. Among their more troubling findings is the fact that a significant percentage of their subjects, in the neighborhood of 25%, have a history of antisocial behavior. Some researchers have reported that adolescents with ADHD consume more alcohol and abuse street drugs more frequently and to a greater extent than do their peers. The Montreal research group, however, found no evidence of alcoholism or significant drug addiction in adulthood as an outcome of the childhood syndrome.

Hyperactive Children Grown Up includes several chapters containing memories, impressions, and comments of the patients themselves. These adults were asked what had helped them most through their lives.

They most often chose a person (a parent, teacher, friend, or counselor) who had believed strongly in them. The majority had not liked taking medicine. They did not like being different or being embarrassed when other children found out. They felt they had not been given enough information about the medicine and the reasons for taking it.

Can some conclusions be drawn from what we have learned? We know that the disorder is wide-ranging and touches all aspects of the lives of those who have it. We know it does not go away. We know it makes growing up difficult and makes living in the family of a child with ADHD hard at times.

On the other hand, we also know that many children with ADHD are able to manage their first jobs well, despite previous school problems. Although many adults have problems, the majority of adults with ADHD lead normal lives.

So, if many children with ADHD manage their first job well, despite problems associated with the syndrome, what guidelines does this suggest for dealing with earlier learning and behavioral problems?

We think three points emerge clearly:

1. Families must get through the difficult times without being torn apart. Protect your family. Guard against hate and rejection. A time may even come for the family when it is best for your child to temporarily live elsewhere. Even if that happens, it can be done constructively and with a minimum of bad feelings. Above all, protect the basic relationships in your family. In a few years, they will again provide the foundation for positive experiences.

2. Protect your child from causing such serious damage to himself or his future that he cannot ever get his life back on track. We have in mind serious crime or drug use. Children can recover from many things, including dropping out of school.

3. Keep self-esteem as high as possible. An important way to do this is to look for ways to implement nonpunitive discipline. Each time you establish an alliance with your child, you strengthen a bond you enjoy and add to the child's sense of worth because she knows you care enough to be an ally. Be strict without being punitive or rejecting in a way that assaults a child's dignity.

There should be a fourth point, but it is so important that it runs through all three of those already listed. Families must learn to maintain a balanced point of view. Essential issues must be sorted from both the inconsequential ones and those that are important but can, without danger, be set aside. It is not necessary to escalate every skipped class, failure to take out the garbage, messy room, or fight with a younger brother to a major confrontation. These tests of will ultimately cause great rancor. Such a course of action can lead to irreparable alienation among family members and a destructive assault on the self-esteem of the child with ADHD.

Where do we go from here? What does the future hold? We can anticipate some future changes and advances that will occur in diagnosis, understanding, and treatment of ADHD. The name of the disorder, attention deficit–hyperactivity disorder, will undoubtedly be changed again as research workers and clinicians strive to define the disorder with greater precision. These efforts to better define and understand the disorder are important but should not deflect your focus from the symptoms of your child or student. The technical definition of ADHD is less important than a thorough understanding of the way in which symptoms are expressed in the learning and behavior of the child or children with whom you work.

In years to come we will certainly find subtypes of ADHD and will come to recognize that the broad-ranging definition of ADHD we now use encompasses a number of subtypes and possibly even discrete disorders. The coming years will also bring increased understanding of the biological basis of ADHD. This will lead to better diagnosis and will help us understand how different types of medication work in alleviating its symptoms.

An important development from the late 1980s is the rapidly increasing parent and community support group movement. Several national coalitions of parent support groups have helped professionals and parents; they also have coalesced into a significant educational and politically active movement that will ensure that the problems of children with ADHD are given the attention and the financial support they deserve by governmental and educational agencies. Everyone concerned with the welfare of children with ADHD should be active in these groups at local, state, and national levels.

In its simplest sense, advice is easy to give but complex and often difficult to put into practice. Be as calm as possible, do not overreact, keep your eye on the future, and use your sense of humor whenever possible. Your child will no doubt survive and go on to live a normal life. Make sure you, as parents, have the same future prospects: a life that will include a mutually rewarding, loving relationship with your adult child.

Rating Scales

The following rating scales can be ordered from the addresses listed.

ADD-H Comprehensive Teacher Rating Scale (*ACT-ers*). Ullmann, R. K., Sleator, E. K., and Sprague, R. L. MetriTech, Inc., 111 N. Market Street, Champaign, IL 61820.

The Child Behavior Checklist, Child Profile, Teacher's Report Form, and *Direct Observation Form.* Dr. Thomas Achenbach, Department of Psychiatry, University of Vermont, 1 South Prospect Street, Burlington, VT 05401.

Teacher and Parent Rating Scales. Conners, C. K. PRO-ED, 8700 Shoal Creek Boulevard, Austin, TX 78758.

Glossary

Most technical words and other terms with which the reader may not be familiar are defined in the text. Included here are shorter definitions for quick reference, as well as a number of other terms frequently encountered by parents and others who work with children with attention deficit–hyperactivity disorder and other learning and behavior problems.

Affect: Moods, feelings, or emotions.

Alexia: Loss of the ability to read written or printed language.

Anoxia: Reduced supply of oxygen for a long enough time to cause brain injury.

Aphasia (dysphasia): Loss or impairment of the ability to understand or formulate language; caused by neurological damage.

Audiogram: A graphic representation of the weakest sound a person can hear at several frequency levels.

Auditory closure: The ability to recognize a whole word or phrase from the presentation of a partial auditory stimulus.

Auditory reception: The ability to derive meaning from orally presented material.

Auditory sequential memory: The ability to remember sequences of auditory stimuli.

Aversive stimulus: A stimulus that a subject will avoid if possible.

Behavior modification: Changing behavior with a variety of techniques based on learning principles, such as conditioning and reinforcement.

Central nervous system: That part of the nervous system to which sensory impulses are transmitted and from which motor impulses originate; the brain and spinal cord.

Cerebral dominance: An assumption that one cerebral hemisphere generally dominates the other in control of bodily movements. In most individuals the left side of the brain controls language and is considered the dominant hemisphere.

Chromosome: One of the bodies in the nucleus of a cell that contains the genes.

Congenital: Present in an individual at birth.

Criterion reference test: A test designed to measure a child's development in terms of absolute levels of mastery, as opposed to measuring the child's status relative to other children, as in a norm reference test.

Diagnostic prescriptive teaching: An educational strategy of delineating a child's strengths and weaknesses and then designing a specific program for teaching on the basis of those findings.

Disinhibition: Lack of ability to refrain from response often resulting in hyperactivity and distractibility.

Distractibility: Being abnormally affected by external stimuli; easily diverted from a task.

Dysarthria: Difficulty in the articulation of words as a result of involvement in the central nervous system.

Dyscalculia: Inability to perform mathematical computations.

Dysgraphia: Inability to produce the motor movements required for handwriting.

Dyslexia: Impairment of the ability to read.

Electroencephalograph: An instrument for recording electrical brain waves.

Emotional lability: Frequent, and often sudden, changes in mood.

Endogenous: Originating from within; a term used to characterize a constitutional condition. (Compare with exogenous.)

Exogenous: Developed or derived from external causes. (Compare with endogenous.)

External locus of control: A personality characteristic in which the individual believes that chance factors or other people are responsible for personal successes and failures.

Extinction: Reduction or elimination of behavior by removing all reinforcement.

Familial: Occurring in members of the same family, as a familial disease.

Figure-ground disturbance: The inability to discriminate a figure from its background.

Gene: Factor responsible for hereditary characteristics, arranged at specific locations in the chromosomes within each cell.

Genetics: The study of heredity.

Genius: A word sometimes used to indicate a particular aptitude or capacity in any area; rare intellectual powers.

Giftedness: Refers to cognitive (intellectual) superiority, creativity, and motivation in combination and of sufficient magnitude to set the child apart from the vast majority of age-mates and make it possible for the child to contribute something of a particular value to society.

Hyperactive: Having excessive movement or motor restlessness.

Hypoglycemia: A condition characterized by abnormally low blood sugar.

Internal locus of control: A personality characteristic in which the individual believes he or she is responsible for personal successes and failures.

IQ (Intelligence Quotient): A measure of intellectual functioning; average IQ is set at 100.

Laterality: Awareness of the two sides of the body and the ability to identify left and right; often used to mean preferential use of one side of the body.

Least restrictive alternative: The philosophy of bringing individuals with disabilities as close to the normal school and social setting as possible.

Mainstreaming: An administrative procedure for keeping exceptional children in the normal classroom for the majority of the school day.

Megavitamin therapy: The use of large doses of vitamins to treat ADHD, learning disabilities, and a number of mental disorders.

Minimal brain dysfunction: A poorly defined syndrome often including hyperactivity, distractibility, perseveration, and disorders of perception, body image, laterality, and sometimes symbolization; not used in this book because of its ambiguity.

Neurology: A medical specialty dealing with the study and treatment of disorders of the nervous system.

Neurophysiological: Pertaining to the physiology of the nervous system.

Organic: Inherent, inborn; involving a known neurological or structural abnormality.

Perception: Refers to an individual's ability to process stimuli meaningfully; the ability to organize and interpret sensory information.

Perceptual-motor impairment: Problems in coordinating a visual or auditory stimulus with a motor act.

Perseveration: Persistent repetition of an activity or a behavior.

Postnatal: After birth.

Prenatal: Before birth.

Proprioceptive: Pertaining to stimulation from the muscles and tendons that gives information concerning the position and movement of the body and its members.

Psychometrics: Refers to standardized psychological tests such as tests of intelligence, perception, and personality.

Psychopathology: The study of the causes and nature of mental disorders.

Receptive language disabilities: Difficulties that derive from the inability to understand spoken language.

Reinforcement: A procedure to strengthen a response by the administration of immediate rewards (positive reinforcement).

Resource teacher: A teacher who typically provides services for the exceptional children and their teachers within one school, assesses the particular needs of such children, and sometimes teaches them individually or in small groups, using any special materials or methods that are needed; he or she consults with regular teachers, advising on the instruction and management of the children in the classroom and demonstrating instructional techniques.

Reticular activating system: A network of neurons that passes through the brain stem. Associated with wakefulness, arousal, and sleep.

Special education: Provision of instruction and supportive services for children with special learning needs.

Special self-contained class: A class that enrolls exceptional children with a particular diagnostic label; usually children within such a class need full-time instruction in this placement and are only integrated with their normal classmates for a few activities, if any.

Stimulus: The physical, chemical, biological, and social events that act on the individual.

Stimulus reduction: A concept largely forwarded by William Cruickshank; an approach to teaching distractible and hyperactive children that emphasizes reducing extraneous (not relevant to learning) material.

Syndrome: A set of characteristics or symptoms that occur together. Attention deficit–hyperactivity disorder is a syndrome.

Sources for Additional Reading

Aarskog, D., Fevang, F. O., Klove, J., Stoa, K., & Thorsen, T. (1977). The effect of the drugs, dextroamphetamine and methylphenidate, on secretion of growth hormone in hyperactive children. *Journal of Pediatrics, 90,* 136–139.

Ackerman, P. T., Dykman, R. A., & Peters, J. E. (1977). Teenage status of hyperactive and non-hyperactive learning disabled boys. *American Journal of Orthopsychiatry, 47,* 577–596.

Alberts-Corush, J., Firestone, P., & Goodman, J. T. (1986). Attention and impulsivity characteristics of the biological and adoptive parents of hyperactive and normal control children. *American Journal of Orthopsychiatry, 56,* 413–423.

American Psychiatric Association. (1987). *Diagnostic and statistical manual mental disorders—DSM III* (3rd ed.). Washington, DC: American Psychiatric Association.

Anastopoulos, A., & Barkley, R. (1988). Biological factors in attention deficit hyperactivity disorder. *Behavioral Therapy, 11,* 47–53.

Atkins, M. S., Pelham, W., & Licht, M. (1985). A comparison of objective classroom measures and teacher ratings of attention deficit disorder. *Journal of Abnormal Child Psychology, 13,* 155–166.

Ballinger, C., Varley, C., & Nolen, P. (1984). Effect of methylphenidate on reading in children with attention deficit disorder. *American Journal of Psychiatry, 141,* 1590–1593.

Barkley, R. (1990). *Attention deficit hyperactivity disorder: A handbook for diagnosis and treatment.* New York: Guilford Press.

Barkley, R., DuPaul, G., & McMurray, M. (1990). Comprehensive evaluation of attention deficit disorder with and without hyperactivity as defined by research criteria. *Journal of Consulting and Clinical Psychology, 58,* 775–789.

Barkley, R., McMurray, M., Edelbrock, C., & Robbins, K. (1990). Side effects of methylphenidate in children with attention deficit hyperactivity disorder: A systematic placebo-control evaluation. *Pediatrics, 86,* 184–192.

Birmaher, B., Watkins, A., & Bielharbor, K. (1989). Sustained release methylphenidate: Pharmacokinetics studies in ADHD males. *Journal of the American Academy of Child and Adolescent Psychiatry, 28,* 768–772.

Brown, R., Wynne, M., & Medenis, R. (1985). Methylphenidate and cognitive therapy: A comparison of treatment approaches of hyperactive boys. *Journal of Abnormal Child Psychology, 13,* 66–73.

Brown, R. T., & Alford, N. (1984). Ameliorating attentional deficits and concomitant academic deficiencies in learning disabled children through cognitive training. *Journal of Learning Disabilities, 17*(1), 20–26.

Brown, R. T., & Sleator, E. K. (1979). Methylphenidate in hyperkinetic children: Differences in dose effects on impulsive behavior. *Pediatrics, 64,* 408–411.

Campbell, A., Breaux, A., Ewing, L., & Szumowski, E. (1986). Correlates and predictives of hyperactivity aggression: A longitudinal study of parent-referred problem preschoolers. *Journal of Abnormal Child Psychology, 14,* 217–227.

Cantwell D., & Baker, R. (1991). Association between attention deficit hyperactivity disorder and learning disorders. *Journal of Learning Disabilities, 24*(2), 88–95.

Charles, L., Schian, R., & Zelniker, T. (1981). Optimal dosages of methylphenidate for improving the learning and behavior of hyperactive children. *Journal of Developmental and Behavioral Pediatrics, 2,* 78–81.

Conners, C. (1980). *Food additives and hyperactive children.* New York: Plenum Press.

Conners, C. K., & Taylor, E. (1980). Pemoline, methylphenidate and placebo in children with minimal brain dysfunction. *Archives of General Psychiatry, 37,* 922–930.

Coward, V. (1988). The Ritalin controversy: What's made this drug's opponents hyperactive? *Journal of the American Medical Association, 259,* 2521–2523.

Denson, R., Nanson, J., & McWatters, M. (1975). Hyperkinesis and maternal smoking. *Canadian Psychiatric Association Journal, 20,* 183–187.

Dulcan, M. (1990). Using psychostimulants to treat behavioral disorders of children and adolescents. *Journal of Child and Adolescent Psychopharmacology, 1,* 7–20.

Epstein, M., Shaywitz, S., Shaywitz, B., & Woolston, J. (1991). The boundaries of attention deficit disorder. *Journal of Learning Disabilities, 24,* 78–86.

Feingold, B. (1974). *Why your child is hyperactive.* New York: Random House.

Firestone, P., Kelly, M., Goodman, J., & Davey, J. (1981). Differential effects of parent training and medication with hyperactives. *Journal of Child Psychiatry, 20,* 135–147.

Firestone, P., Kelly, M., Goodman, J., & Davey, J. (1986). Differential effects of parent training and stimulant medication with hyperactives. *American Journal of Orthopsychiatry, 56,* 184–194.

Furukawa, C. P., Shapiro, G., Du Hamel, T., Weimer, I., Pierson, W., & Bierman, C. (1984). Learning and behavior problems associated with theophylline therapy. *Lancet, 1,* 621.

Goldstein, S., & Goldstein, M. (1990). *Managing attention disorders in children.* New York: Wiley.

Gordon, M. (1991). *ADHD/hyperactivity: A consumer's guide*. DeWitt, NY: GSI Publications.

Harsough, C., & Lambert, N. (1985). Medical factors in hyperactive and normal children: Prenatal, development and health history findings. *American Journal of Orthopsychiatry, 52*, 190–201.

Holborow, P., & Berry, P. (1986). A multinational, cross-cultural perspective on hyperactivity. *American Journal of Orthopsychiatry, 56*(2), 320–322.

Howell, D. (1985). Fifteen-year follow-up of behavioral history of attention deficit disorder. *Pediatrics, 76*, 185–189.

Johnston, M., & Singer, H. (1982). Brain neurotransmitter and neuromodulators in pediatrics. *Pediatrics, 70*, 57–69.

Klee, S., Garfinkel, B., & Beauchesne, H. (1986). Attention deficits in adults. *Psychiatric Annals, 16*(1), 52–56.

Kupietz, S., Winsberg, B., & Sverd, J. (1982). Learning ability and methylphenidate (Ritalin) plasma concentration in hyperkinetic children. *Journal of Child Psychiatry, 21*, 27–30.

McGee, R., & Share, D. (1988). Attention deficit hyperactivity disorder and academic failure: Which comes first and what should be treated? *Journal of the American Academy of Child and Adolescent Psychiatry, 27*, 318–325.

Margolis, H., Brannigan, G. G., & Poston, M. A. (1977). Modification of impulsivity: Implications for teaching. *Elementary School Journal, 77*, 231–237.

Mattes, J., Boswell, L., & Oliver, H. (1984). Methylphenidate effects on symptoms of attention deficit disorder in adults. *Archives of General Psychiatry, 41*, 1059–1067.

Milich, R., & Pelham, W. (1986). Effects of sugar ingested on the classroom and playgroup behavior of attention deficit disordered boys. *Journal of Consulting Clinical Psychology, 54*, 714–718.

O'Leary, S. G., & Pelham, W. E. (1978). Behavioral therapy withdrawal of stimulant medication in hyperactive children. *Pediatrics, 61*, 211–217.

Palfrey, J., Levine, M., Walker, D., & Sullivan, M. (1985). The emergence of attention deficit in early childhood. A prospective study. *Journal of Developmental and Behavioral Pediatrics, 6*, 339–348.

Parker, H. (1988). *The ADD hyperactivity workbook*. Plantation, FL: Impact Publications.

Pelham, W., Greenslade, M., Vodde-Hamilton, M., Murphy, D., Greenstein, J., Gagny, E., & Guthrie, K. (1990). Relative efficacy of long acting stimulants on children with attention deficit hyperactivity disorder: A comparison of standard methylphenidate, sustained release methylphenidate, sustained release Dextroamphetamine and Pemoline. *Pediatrics, 86*, 226–236.

Rachelefsky, G., Wo, J., Adelson, J., Mickey, M., Spector, S., Katz, R., & Siegel, S. (1986, December). Behavior abnormalities and poor school performance due to oral theophylline use. *Pediatrics, 78*, 1133–1138.

Rapoport, J. (1978). Dextro-amphetamine: Cognitive and behavioral effects in normal prepubertal boys. *Science, 199*, 560–562.

Rapport, M., DuPaul, G., Stoner, G., & Jones, T. (1985). Attention deficit disorder with hyperactivity: Differential effects of methylphenidate on impulsivity. *Pediatrics, 76,* 938–943.

Richardson, E., Kupietz, S., Winsberg, B., & Maitinsky, S. (1988). Effects of methylphenidate dosage in hyperactive reading disabled children: II. Reading achievement. *Journal of the American Academy of Child and Adolescent Psychiatry, 27,* 78–87.

Ross, D. M., & Ross, S. A. (1982). *Hyperactivity: Current issues, research and theory* (2nd ed.). New York: Wiley-Interscience.

Rourke, B. (1976). Issues in the neuropsychological assessment of children with learning disabilities. *Canadian Psychological Review, 17,* 89–102.

Safer, D., & Krager, M. (1983). Trends in medication treatment of school children. *Clinical Pediatrics, 22,* 500–504.

Satterfield, J. H., Satterfield, B. T., & Kentwell, D. (1981). Three-year multimodality treatment study of 100 hyperactive boys. *Pediatrics, 73,* 650–655.

Schain, C. L. (1981). A four year follow up study of the effects of methylphenidate on the behavior and academic achievement of hyperactive children. *Journal of Abnormal Child Psychology, 9,* 495–505.

Shaywitz, S., Hunt, R., Jatlow, P., Cohen, D., Young, J., Pierce, R., & Anderson, G. (1982). Psychopharmacology of attention deficit disorders: Pharmacokinetic, neuroendocrine, and behavioral measures following acute and chronic treatment with methylphenidate. *Pediatrics, 69,* 688–694.

Silver, L. (1975). Acceptable and controversial approaches to treating the child with learning disabilities. *Pediatrics, 55,* 406–415.

Sprague, R. L., & Sleator, E. K. (1975). What is the proper dose of stimulant drugs in children? *International Journal of Mental Health, 4,* 75–105.

Sprague, R. L., & Sleator, E. K. (1977). Methylphenidate in hyperkinetic children: Differences in dose effects on learning and social behavior. *Science, 198,* 1274–1276.

Stewart, M. A., Mendelson, W. B., & Johnson, N. E. (1984). Hyperactive children as adolescents: How they describe themselves. *Child Psychiatry and Human Development, 7,* 31–38.

Swanson, J., Cantwell, D., Lerner, M., McBurnett, K., & Hanna, G. (1991). Effects of stimulant medication on learning and children with ADHD. *Journal of Learning Disabilities, 24,* 219–230.

Swanson, J. M., & Kinsbourne, M. (1980). Food dyes impair performance of hyperactive children on laboratory learning test. *Science, 207,* 1485.

Tryphonas, H., & Trites, R. (1979). Food allergy in children with hyperactivity, learning disabilities, and/or minimal brain dysfunction. *Annals of Allergy, 42,* 22–27.

Weery, J., Reeves, J., & Elkind, G. (1987). Attention deficit, conduct, oppositional and anxiety disorders in children: I. A review of research on differentiating characteristics. *Journal of the American Academy of Child and Adolescent Psychiatry, 26,* 133–145.

Weiss, B., Williams, J. H., Margen, S., Abrams, B., Caan, B., Citron, L., Cox, C., & McKibben, J. (1980). Behavioral responses to artificial food colors. *Science, 207,* 1487.

Weiss, G., & Hechtman, L. (1986). *Hyperactive children grown up.* New York: Guilford Press.

Wender, P. (1986). The food additive–free diet in the treatment of behavior disorders: A review. *Journal of Developmental and Behavioral Pediatrics, 7,* 35–42.

Woolfolk, A. E., & Woolfolk, R. L. (1974). A contingency management technique for increasing student attention in a small group setting. *Journal of School Psychology, 12,* 204–212.

Professional and Parent Organizations

Listed below are the names and addresses of societies, organizations, and agencies serving families and children with special needs. Many can supply additional information and material that you may find useful.

Allergy Foundation of America
801 Second Avenue
New York, NY 10017

American Association of Psychiatric Clinics for Children
Room 1032
250 West 57th Street
New York, NY 10019

American Foundation on Learning Disabilities
P.O. Box 196
Convent Station, NJ 07961

Attention Deficit Disorders Association (ADDA)
8091 South Ireland Way
Aurora, CO 80016

Children with Attention Deficit Disorders (CHADD)
Suite 185
1859 North Pine Island Road
Plantation, FL 33322

Council for Exceptional Children
1920 Association Drive
Reston, VA 22091

Family Service Association of America
44 East 23rd Street
New York, NY 10010

Foundation for Attentional Disorders
Box 339 Station "D"
Toronto, Ontario M6P 3J9
Canada

Foundation for Child Development
345 East 46th Street
New York, NY 10017

Learning Disability Association (LDA)
4156 Library Road
Pittsburgh, PA 15234
(Affiliate organizations in all states)

National Association for Mental Health
10 Columbus Circle
New York, NY 10019

National Information Center for the Handicapped
P.O. Box 1492
Washington, DC 20013

National Rehabilitation Association
1522 K Street N.W.
Washington, DC 20005

U.S. Office of Education Bureau of Education for the Handicapped
400 Maryland Avenue S.W.
Washington, DC 20202

U.S. Office of Vocational Education
400 Maryland Avenue S.W.
Washington, DC 20202

Index

Attention Deficit Disorder: A Workshop for Psychologists, Social Workers, Teachers, Counselors, and Parents. Presented by Doyal, Friedman & Associates and Ronald J. Friedman, PhD.

Dr. Friedman, coauthor of *Management of Children and Adolescents with Attention Deficit–Hyperactivity Disorder, Third Edition,* is available to present either a half-day or a full-day workshop in your area for professionals and/or parents. The program can be developed to fit the needs of your particular community. For further information write:

Ronald J. Friedman, PhD
19900 Ten Mile Road
St. Clair Shores, MI 48081

Phone: (313) 776-2949

pro·ed

8700 Shoal Creek Boulevard
Austin, Texas 78757

Order Number 4038

ISBN 0-89079-532-0